New Orleans con Sabor Latino

The History and Passion of Latino Cooking

NEW ORLEANS
con Sabor Latino

Zella Palmer Cuadra   Photography by Natalie Root

University Press of Mississippi / Jackson

www.upress.state.ms.us

The University Press of Mississippi is a member
of the Association of American University Presses.

Designed by Todd Lape

Copyright © 2013 by University Press of Mississippi
Photographs © 2013 by Natalie Root
Printed in China by Everbest through
Four Colour Imports, Ltd., Louisville, Kentucky

First printing 2013

∞

Library of Congress Cataloging-in-Publication Data

Cuadra, Zella Palmer.
New Orleans con sabor Latino : the history and passion of
Latino cooking / Zella Palmer Cuadra ; photographs by Natalie
Root.
pages cm
In English.
Includes bibliographical references and index.
ISBN 978-1-61703-895-2 (hardback) — ISBN 978-1-61703-896-9
(ebook) 1. Cooking, American—Louisiana style. 2. Cooking—
Louisiana—New Orleans—History. 3. Cooking, Latin American.
4. Hispanic Americans—Louisiana—New Orleans. I. Title.
TX715.2.L68C83 2013
641.59763'35—dc23   2013015041

British Library Cataloging-in-Publication Data available

To Mur, Evelyn, Norma, Yanetsy, Wilber
"El Gran Cocinero," Maria, Alexis, Yanoxy,
San Jhon, the communities of Humboldt Park
and South Chicago, my parents, Liz Williams,
and in memory of University of Toronto
Museum Studies Professor Cheryl Meszaros

Contents

**STORIES AND RECIPES FROM THE
NEW ORLEANS LATINO COMMUNITY**

LAGNIAPPE

Foreword

New Orleans always takes the best of people's culture, be it African, French, Spanish, Italian, German, or Caribbean, and Latinos are considered the new wave of immigrants coming to the city. Latinos came to New Orleans during the 1800s when there were revolutions in Cuba and Haiti, and Cubans then came again in the 1940s way before Fidel Castro entered the world stage. Mexicans also came to New Orleans before the Mexican War (1846–1848). Latinos historically were drawn to New Orleans to make a better life for their families and due to the fact that New Orleans was, and still is, a port city so close to home.

However, for me as a Latino growing up in NOLA, it was kind of a unique situation. My development as a Latino was not all or nothing. I knew I was Latino because in my house we all spoke Spanish and the neighbors spoke English and/or French. Although my parents were Panamanian, our governess, as she liked to be called, was Go Go of Honduran origin. She was like a mother to us, but I knew she was different from my parents culturally, in a subtle way. Her accent was different. The way she said *chumpa* for *abrigo* and the way she cooked beans with tortillas made her totally different from my parents with their Caribbean culture.

When I was a child, there were pockets of Latino communities on Magazine Street in the late 1960s and throughout the 1970s. There was a theatre there that would show *Cantinflas,* and I would go with my parents and their friends. There was a Honduran restaurant that made delicious Honduran-style corn, *platanos maduros*, and rice and beans. My best friend Mario's dad owned a club called The Latin American, and everyone went there to dance, socialize, and eat. However, the center of Latin culture in New Orleans was La Union Super Mercado, which was next to Rock and Bowl. My mom would go there to buy *chicharrónes, jugo de guanabana, platanos maduros y verdes*. As I grew older, I realized that each one of our Latin American countries has different subtleties—the accent, the food, and the music—but we are all still connected. I started seeing the similarities instead of the differences in our cultures.

When I started grade school there weren't many olive- or brown-skinned people in my school or neighborhood. Looking back on my childhood, I realize that I didn't learn until later that New Orleans red beans and rice is as integral to our cuisine as it is in Latin America. Interestingly, this does not apply to the rest of the South. Being Latino and raised in New Orleans, I thought everybody ate red beans and rice. It just happened that in my house we ate them every day as my neighbors did. To me food is our common ground as Panamanians, Dominicans, Mexicans, Cubans, and so forth. We identify and distinguish ourselves by our food. I enjoy seeing how our culture in NOLA continues to be influenced by our Latino roots. It is undeniable that New Orleans cuisine was influenced by the Spanish with dishes like jambalaya and the famous king cake, or *rosca de reyes*. Then of course the soulfulness of Haiti and Cuba are undeniably present in the greatest assets of NOLA, the food and the music. New Orleans would not be what it is today without the influences of the Latin and Caribbean cultures brought by our people. So when you see Hondurans and Dominicans boiling crawfish as part of their cookouts, or New Orleans natives eating *pupusas* or Cuban sandwiches, it is not that unusual anymore. We just keep on adding to the gumbo of this city we call New Orleans.

Since I decided to become a chef I wanted to bring these worlds together. So when someone looks at my avocado remoulade they might see guacamole, but I never ate guacamole. We didn't really have Mexican food in New Orleans. To me guacamole is what American people ate in Ohio. When I look at a remoulade it is a chunky sauce that is served with seafood that has certain ingredients, and avocado is an integral part of what we eat in Latin America. To somebody in Thailand it doesn't look like either one of those; it looks like something they make. So really it depends on how you look at it.

Case in point, if you served New Orleans barbecue shrimp in Memphis, people would say this is not barbecue shrimp. But stand on the corner of South Peters and Julia Street in New Orleans and they would say that's barbecue shrimp. It's all about the interpretation of culture. So when Zella Palmer Cuadra came into my restaurant in the summer of 2009 with her idea I most definitely wanted to be a part of it. This book is written by a young lady with a deep passion and understanding of the uniqueness of New Orleans culture. And because of her Latin perspective, she has the ability to identify and clarify the Latin influences that give texture to this being we call New Orleans. Her perspective is revealing and unique. It is a great piece of work to help you and me understand why Latin culture matters in New Orleans.

Zella, I met you as a struggling grad student with a dream to highlight our common culture as

an important and relevant influence in the NOLA
that is my home, and it took your sensitivity and
passion to teach me and the readers of this work
what it means to be Latin in NOLA.

—Chef Adolfo Garcia

About the Book

New Orleans con Sabor Latino: The History and Passion of Latino Cooking is a documentary cookbook that draws on the rich Latino culture and history of New Orleans by focusing on thirteen New Orleanian Latinos from diverse backgrounds. Their stories are compelling and reveal a rich history that for too long has been overlooked. The book also celebrates the influence of Latino cuisine on the food culture of New Orleans from the early nineteenth century to the influx of Latino migration post-Katrina to New Orleans today. Finally, the cookbook includes a lagniappe (something extra) section of New Orleans recipes from a Latin perspective by the author. For the interviews, Zella Palmer Cuadra visited and interviewed each participant. The dishes are placed in historical context. This is an important book for the history of the city of New Orleans, for culinary history in the city, and for culinary history nationwide. Very few scholars or writers have devoted as much attention to New Orleans Spanish heritage as has been given to French heritage. Nor has attention been paid to the many different origins of the Spanish-speaking people who, from the early 1700s to the present, have contributed to the identity of the city. This book, the first to place this influence in terms of cooking, is a landmark in New Orleans history itself.

Acknowledgments

During the summer of 2009, I was a museum studies graduate student at the University of Toronto, completing my internship at the Southern Food & Beverage Museum in New Orleans, Louisiana. The director of SoFAB, Liz Williams, assigned me to work in the museum collections vault to research and curate an online exhibit called *Tremé's Cooking: The Culinary Legacy of Tremé.* I spent months researching the culinary history of New Orleans and the culinary influences of the Tremé neighborhood. While conducting my research I couldn't help but notice how limited the information was on the Spanish, or Latino, culinary history and its influence on Louisiana cuisine. Yet so much of New Orleans's cuisine to me was like a distant relative to Latin American cuisine. As a native Chicagoan, a city that is heavily influenced by Latino culture and cuisine, naturally I gravitated towards what I know and my own cultural memories.

In the midst of my research for SoFAB, my beloved University of Toronto professor Cheryl Meszaros died. My classmates and I who were scattered across the world interning in different museums were devastated. I went back to Toronto in the fall of 2009 after completing my internship at SoFAB saddened that I wouldn't be able to share my research and experiences with her. The post-Katrina 2010 Saints victory, which I watched from my basement apartment in Toronto, and the joyousness that swept the city nudged me to return to New Orleans to continue my work and to honor my professor.

I would especially like to thank all of my classmates at the University of Toronto who bought my gumbo at fund-raisers outside of the Faculty of Information Studies library to help raise funds for me to come back to New Orleans.

This book would not have been possible without Natalie Root Photography. Thank you for coming into the museum that day and sharing this amazing journey with me.

Thanks go to Liz Williams at the Southern Food & Beverage Museum for her guidance and mentoring during this project, to Edgar Sierra Jimenez for his photographs, history lessons, and hospitality, and to Chef Adolfo Garcia of Rio Mar for delivering on his offer: "Whatever you need, baby."

I am grateful for Tia Vice's direction and research input, to Franklin Sanchez for his humor, support, and love for New Orleans during the initial stages of this project, to Victor Payan, Director of Programs at the National Association of Latino Arts and Culture during our initial grant application, to Chef John Folse for interviewing me on his radio program, to Yolanda Estrada, WWOZ radio show host of *Tiene Sabor* for interviewing me after the launch of the *New Orleans con Sabor Latino* culinary exhibit at the Southern Food & Beverage Museum, and to Alberta Lewis for connecting me with the Isleños community. I am also grateful to the Martins, who helped me get primary resources and who sent e-mail correspondences encouraging me to have mustard-seed faith during this project.

I appreciate the librarians at the New Orleans Public Library, the New Orleans Historic Collection, and the Beatrice Rodriguez Owsley Collection at Earl K. Long Library at the University of New Orleans. I am grateful to Director Hortensia Calvo of the Tulane Latin American Library for her wisdom and research expertise, to LatiNola, which allowed me to volunteer in the community, and to Rafael Delgadillo, who shared his knowledge and commitment to the Latino community in New Orleans. I would also like to give special mention to Latino Farmers Cooperative of Louisiana, United Dominicans of Louisiana, ¿Que Pasa New Orleans?, Ana de la Garza at the Mexican Consulate, and the Hispanic Apostolate of New Orleans for their grassroots work in the Latino community of greater New Orleans—all organizations that I have worked closely with in some capacity. Finally, this book is dedicated to the Latino community of greater New Orleans both past and present.

Note: *New Orleans con Sabor Latino* photo documentary exhibit ran from August 28, 2010, to November 15, 2010, at the Southern Food & Beverage Museum in New Orleans. It was curated by Zella Palmer Cuadra and photographed by Natalie Root. Culinary programming included many of the participants in the exhibit.

New Orleans con Sabor Latino

Introduction

In a chapter on the Spanish Period in their book *Beautiful Crescent: A History of New Orleans* (1988), authors Joan B. Garvey and Mary Lou Widmer stated, "The City of New Orleans was *never* Spanish, in its customs, culture, or language. Throughout the period of Spanish domination, it remained tenaciously French. The French language was spoken in schools and in business. There was never a Spanish newspaper printed in the city. The people of New Orleans never became Spanish speaking people until the Cubans began arriving in the 1960s."

My friend and colleague Rafael Delgadillo dispelled Garvey and Widmer's argument in his master's thesis for the University of New Orleans History Department, "A 'Spanish' Element in the New South: The Hispanic Press and Community in 19th Century New Orleans" (2009). His extensive research proved that the Spanish did have influence on the city of New Orleans with their introduction of the term *lagniappe*, a system or practice where customers were given a little extra when they purchased something from retailers; *coatarcion,* which allowed blacks to purchase

their freedom and hence to develop a community of free people of color; the immigration of at least two thousand Canary Islanders called the *Isleños* who indeed did speak Spanish and had an impact on the culture of Louisiana. Delgadillo proved that New Orleans did in fact have a Spanish newspaper called *El Misisipi,* which was published in 1808. Since *El Misisipi,* Spanish-language newspapers have existed in every decade to this day in New Orleans. Interestingly, prior to the Civil War, twenty-three Spanish-language periodicals were printed, making New Orleans "the capital of Hispanophone print production." New York only had thirteen.

The Garvey and Widmer argument that "The people of New Orleans never became Spanish speaking people until the Cubans began arriving in the 1960s" completely ignores history and the evidence that Latinos have been here since the eighteenth century. The city of New Orleans is right at the Gulf of México and is surrounded by México, Central America, and Cuba, which also means, according to countless records, that trade between Latin America and New Orleans ports was continuous throughout the eighteenth, nineteenth, and twentieth centuries.

Not only did New Orleans import food and items from Latin America; the city also housed many political exiles and Latino immigrants. As early as 1760, Mexicans were living in New Orleans, and Cubans came during the nineteenth century. Remnants of their existence in New Orleans can be seen in the many statues paying tribute to the fathers of Latin American independence throughout the city, such as the one of Benito Juárez, former president of México and one of the forefathers of Mexican independence. Juárez worked in cigar factories and lived in New Orleans between 1853 and 1855; a statue of him can be found in the Tremé Garden on Basin and Conti. Rumor has it that Benito Juárez sold fish in the famous French Market. During his exile in New Orleans, he drafted the Plan of Ayutla—a call for a Mexican revolution.

Simón Bolivar, known as *El Libertador* (The Liberator) of South America, was rumored to have visited New Orleans. His statue can be seen on Canal Street. In 1884, exiled Cuban leaders Antonio Maceo and Máximo Gomez, who were responsible for Cuba's independence from Spain, rented a house at 227 St. Phillip in the Faubourg Tremé. Cubans were constantly coming and going in New Orleans during the nineteenth century. Kirsten Silva Gruez gives New Orleans the title *El Paris Hispano* (The Hispanic Paris) in the book *Ambassadors of Culture: The Transamerican Origins of Latino Writing* (2002). Gruez refers to New Orleans as a place where intellectuals, political exiles, and elites came either to visit or immigrate in the nineteenth century. Gruez said: "Expatriates and émigrés from around the Caribbean and Spanish America would have found New Orleans the least alienating city in the nation—for, besides the substantial population of Spanish speakers, most of their educated classes knew French and could get by without speaking a word of English." Given this history, it is troubling that the book *Beautiful Crescent,* which questions this history, is used as the study manual for an exam New Orleans tour guides must take to be licensed. The book is known as the "bible for tour guides" in New Orleans.

To get an understanding of the Spanish and Latino culinary histories in New Orleans we must first look at Louisiana when the Spanish, the first Latin immigrants to New Orleans, ruled, and see Spain's contribution to the culinary scene in New Orleans. In the foreword to *New Orleans Cuisine: Fourteen Signature Dishes and Their Histories* (2009), Susan Tucker said, "The Spanish flavors associated with the slow sautéing of onions, bell peppers, garlic, and seasoning became a fundamental part of the city's foods." Spanish culinary influences can be seen in many of New Orleans's famous dishes. The Spaniards' love for everything pork can be seen in the variations of sausage making (*chaurice* similar to *chorizo*) and *cochinillo asado,* or slow roasted suckling pig. Another classic New Orleans dish is jambalaya; although the origin of jambalaya is disputed, one can argue that it bears a striking resemblance to the Spanish *paella*. Furthermore, the Mardi Gras king cake, or *rosca de reyes,* was brought by both the French and the Spanish, while the mirliton, or *chayote,* used in Creole and Cajun cuisine was brought from México by the Spanish into New Orleans. The Spanish were also responsible for the organization, regulation, and establishment of open-air markets in New Orleans that allowed its residents and vendors to have access to an abundance of food. Lafcadio Hearn, a noted culinary historian during the late nineteenth century, in his book *La Cuisine Creole* (1885) reveals that ham, a Spanish food staple, was used in many gumbo recipes in New Orleans before sausage was introduced to gumbo.

Another cultural group that must be recognized is that of the Canary Islanders, or Isleños, who were mostly farmers and fisherman summoned by the Spanish during the American Revolution. The Isleños supplied New Orleans commercial markets with their wares. Their culinary legacy can be seen at their annual Isleños festival in St. Bernard Parish with mouth-watering dishes such as *croquettas,* meat pies, *platanos Isleños,* Canary Island shrimp, and *paella*.

There are other such culinary influences. The Mexican capsicum peppers would be found in nearly every cupboard of the city, in a bottle of hot sauce, whose makers always credited a returning soldier from the Mexican War (1846–1848). Tabasco has been the number-one hot sauce in the United States since World War II; it was named for the city of Tabasco in México.

We must also understand that New Orleans's geographical location played an integral role in culinary history as a bridge between New Orleans and Latin America and the Caribbean. Kirsten Silva Gruez said in her book *Ambassadors of Culture,* "Midcentury New Orleans was fundamentally a Caribbean city, strategically positioned within the transportation and communication system of the Gulf of México's half-moon, linked to Cuba, Puerto Rico, Santo Domingo, and México's Gulf Coast and Yucatán." It then would be logical to assume that if Latinos were coming into New Orleans as political exiles or seamen or were brought to New Orleans as the Mexicans were and New Orleans served as a central hub for rum, food, and other items from Latin America, then the culinary influences on New Orleans should also have come from Latin American countries in the Gulf of México.

A case in point is that shrimp Creole, a classic New Orleans dish that was brought to the city by émigrés from Haiti during the Haitian revolution, is almost identical to Cuban shrimp Creole. Many Haitians stopped and lived in Santiago, Cuba, before coming to New Orleans, so it is possible that Haitians left Cuba with new culinary varieties. Also, the famous red beans and rice was brought to New Orleans during this same time period from Haiti. Red beans and rice is also prepared in the Dominican Republic, the neighbor of Haiti, and the dish is called *La Bandera Dominicana*, the Dominican Flag. Red beans and rice is also found in Central America, and there is a variation in México. Evidence of Latino culinary influences on nineteenth-century New Orleans cuisine can be found in *The Picayune's Creole Cook Book* (1901), which includes a recipe for tamales using the term Mexican-Creole.

In the twentieth century many Latinos came to New Orleans as political exiles, students, workers, and, in the case of the Hondurans, via the United Fruit Company. *Lucero Latino* (1934), a New Orleans publication for elite Latin Americans living in the city of New Orleans, included ads for a Honduran restaurant called Restaurante Honduras, for a Creole restaurant that appears to openly welcome Latinos called Restaurant de la Casa Holmes, for a Honduran beverage company called La Famosa Imperial, known for selling ginger ale and African cola, and finally, a back cover ad that entices Latinos to travel on United Fruit Company's Great White Fleet.

An economically diverse group of immigrants from Latin America was living in New Orleans during the nineteenth and twentieth centuries, and they were eating food that was available to their socioeconomic class. For the book *Storyville, New Orleans, Being an Authentic, Illustrated Account of the Notorious Red-Light District* (1974), in 1961 Al Rose interviewed Lola, a woman from the Dominican Republic who married in Santo Domingo at the age of sixteen. Lola was brought to New Orleans in 1911 but was abandoned within a year of her arrival. She was a working girl at the infamous May Spencer's brothel. Lola gives a vivid account of how May Spencer fed all the working girls well with meat, fruit, vegetables, water, milk, French bread, coffee, and po'boy sandwiches.

Maybe t'ree o'clock in de mawning, we eat. Ees good comida in May Spencer house. Ees always bes' meat, fruit, vegetables—all you wan'! Plenny bawtter; plenny meelk. Some time we go hongry before dat, we sen' street boy to Toro for po'-boy sanweech. Ees always lee'l boy in street, dey run faw you. He breeng po'-boy sanweech, I pay heem (Rose, 164).

Luis Adam Nazario of Puerto Rico studied at Tulane University during the 1930s, and years later in 1974 he published a book called *Mi Vida Estudiantil en Nueva Orleans (My Student Life in New Orleans)*. Though his funds were low in his student days, when he treated himself he and his girlfriend would eat at Antoine's, a restaurant that reminded him of La Mallorquina in Old San Juan. *"Comer en Antoine's es comer bien . . . no solamente para comer, si que tambien para converser sobre negocios, condiciones culturales y sociales."* ("Eating at Antoine's means eating well . . . Not only is it suitable to eat but to converse over business, cultural and social conditions.")

Norman Wellington Painter's 1949 Tulane University thesis, "The Assimilation of Latin Americans in New Orleans," includes detailed interviews with over ten participants about their adjustments to eating New Orleans cuisine. Some recent immigrants reported their initial distaste for New Orleans cuisine, how they missed their native food, and how ingredients to make their native food were "too hard to get." However, others said the food was about the same and they enjoyed many New Orleans dishes. Wellington further explains that because New Orleans never developed an isolated community for Latinos like, say, New York immigrant enclaves did, food preparation for Latino immigrants was born out of a lack of access to native ingredients, pockets of Latino communities, and an eventual assimilation into the mainstream culture. In his closing argument, Wellington Painter says, "The food in New Orleans is more similar to that of the subject people than the food in our northern industrial cities. Some of the informants have been in the North and described the food there as 'tasteless' and 'flat.'" One interviewee stated, "I had no difficulty adjusting to the food here. When I go to other places in the United States I miss the food in New Orleans because the other food is not seasoned as well as that in New Orleans."

Today, Latinos in New Orleans are still considered to be pockets of a community and have yet to make a huge impact on the culinary world of New Orleans. However, each culture that came to New Orleans or Louisiana gave the best of its cuisine to the city and is a reflection of the American fabric of many cultures contributing to one pot of gumbo.

Latino culinary history must be included in the making of New Orleans cuisine. When I came to New Orleans in 2009 as a graduate student intern at the Southern Food & Beverage Museum, I was surprised after much research in historic cookbooks and history books how little, if any, mention is made of the Latino presence in New Orleans. I found this to be strange when New Orleans is in such close proximity to Latin America and is a city that bears a striking resemblance to the architecture, music, and food of Latin America. After extensive research, I found that New Orleans does have a rich Latino culinary history that needs to be recognized and celebrated. It is not my intention in writing this book to minimize other cultures that make up the gumbo of Louisiana; rather, this book calls attention to an area that has not been researched in as much detail as it deserves: the culinary history of Latinos in New Orleans both past and present. I also wanted members of the Latino community to speak for themselves and tell their stories about the city they love through their food.

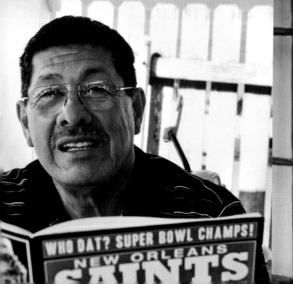

STORIES AND RECIPES FROM THE

NEW ORLEANS LATINO COMMUNITY

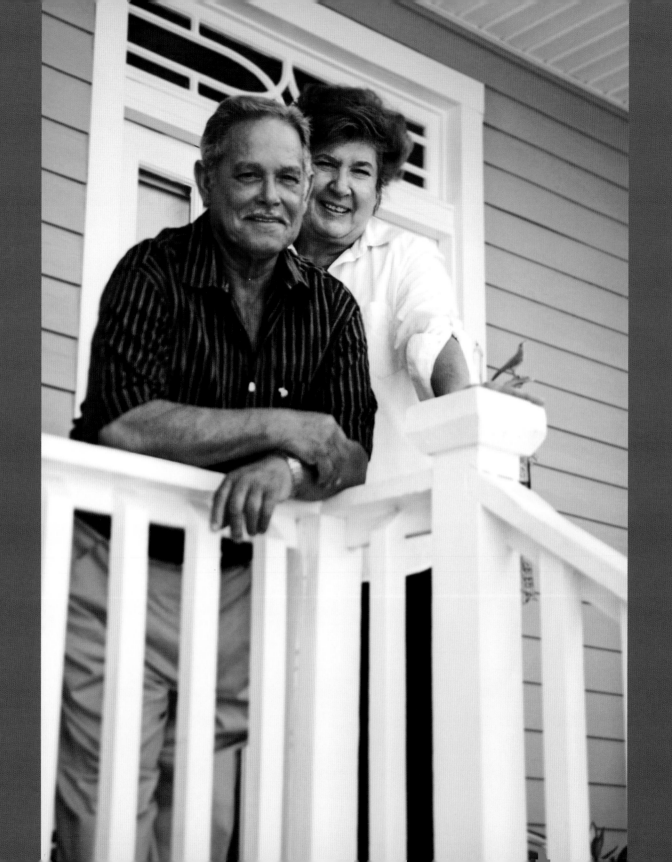

MIKE AND DONNA MARTIN

Mike Martin (April 30, 1941, St. Bernard Parish), a retired port captain for twenty-seven years and a carpenter, was born at his family home in St. Bernard Parish, a historic Isleños community. Mike's father, Andre Martin, came from a small fishing village of three hundred people in Granada, Spain. After fighting against the Franco regime, he left Spain and moved to New Orleans, where he married a woman of French and Canary Island descent, Mike's mother. They had six children.

We were poor back then and there was no such thing as a free lunch for poor kids. I came to school every day with a piece of bread and a whole fish. Even though we were poor we always had plenty of food, and they never wasted anything. We ate a lot of garbanzos and bacalao. We ate some good stuff, caldo, lots of fish, shrimp, crab, ducks, deer, animals that you can hunt like rabbit. Isleños eat a lot of rabbit.

Donna Maria Phillips Martin (January 14, 1944, New Orleans) was born at Old Mercy Hospital in New Orleans and grew up in St. Bernard Parish.

Donna has fond memories of her mother, grandmother, and aunts sipping coffee in the kitchen and gossiping in Spanish.

The kitchen was the heart of the home. I was an only child, but I had tons of cousins. It was a ritual. Standard Coffee would deliver coffee to our door and my dad roasted and ground the coffee and chicory. My mama would make the coffee and always add a dash of salt. Then my dad would go hunting in the marshlands with his double-barrel shotgun. Back then people killed animals to put food on the table, not for sport. They respected the land and we never wasted whatever was caught for the day.

Before Katrina, Mike began building a picturesque plantation-style home for his future bride in a lush area of St. Bernard Parish. The house was nearly destroyed during Katrina. It took Mike many years to rebuild the wedding gift he constructed with his own hands for his wife, Donna. Today they spend their days reminiscing about days gone by, children who have moved away in

search of work, and the reality of Mike's loss of income after the BP oil spill in 2010.

In the summer of 2010, the morning of the photo shoot, Mike went out on his boat in a secluded area untouched by the oil spill to catch a redfish for our feast. While preparing the red-fish, he had a moment of sadness as he realized the impact of the tragic oil spill on a fishing tradi-tion and way of life of more than two hundred years for the Isleños. Although saddened by the recent damage to the fishing culture on the Gulf of Mexico, Mike and Donna continue to cook with the freshest ingredients from their garden, fish as often as possible, and entertain their guests in their beautiful home.

Corvina Roja con Salsa Roja Isleña y Arroz con Leche
Baked Redfish with Isleños Tomato Gravy

Makes about 4 servings: 30 minutes prep time, 1 hour cooking time

Ingredients
2 tablespoons of olive or vegetable oil
2 medium onions, finely chopped
1½ cups of green bell pepper, diced
1 stalk of celery, finely chopped
3 cloves of garlic, minced
2 tablespoons of fresh Italian parsley, minced

1 teaspoon of fresh oregano, minced
1 teaspoon of fresh thyme, minced
1 30-ounce can of tomato sauce
1 15-ounce can of diced tomatoes
1½ cups water or 1½ cups of fish stock
1 whole redfish or Louisiana drum fish*
1 teaspoon of salt and freshly ground pepper
A dash of hot sauce to taste
4 medium potatoes, quartered
Garnish with fresh parsley, chives, and sliced lemons

*Any type of fish can be used, but preferably whole redfish or drum. Clean and scale fish. Rub with salt and pepper. Set aside. Preheat oven to 375 degrees.

Preparation
In a 6-quart sauce pot heat olive oil. Sauté onions, bell pepper, and celery until onions are translucent. Add garlic, parsley, oregano, and thyme and sauté for 2–3 minutes. Add diced tomatoes and cook for 5 minutes. Add the tomato sauce and 1½ cups of water or fish stock. Simmer sauce on low-to-medium heat for approximately 35–40 minutes.

Place fish and quartered potatoes in large baking pan; pour sauce over and around fish and potatoes.

Cook fish and potatoes until the fish flakes, approximately 40 minutes. Do not overcook the fish. If the fish is cooked and the potatoes aren't, remove fish from the pan and cook pota-toes for additional 10 minutes.

Remove from oven and place fish and potatoes on a large platter. Garnish with fresh chopped chives, whole parsley, and sliced lemon. Serve with cooked white rice.

Arroz con Leche
Rice Pudding

Makes about 8–10 large servings: 15 minutes prep time, 30–40 minutes cooking time

Ingredients

2¼ cups of medium-grain uncooked rice

½ cup of rum, preferably spice rum

½ cup of raisins

7 cups of whole milk

1 cup of half-and-half

1 tablespoon of vanilla extract

½ teaspoon of salt

½ teaspoon of cinnamon

4 egg yolks

2 whole eggs

2 cups of sugar

Zest of 1 lemon

Preparation

Rinse rice until the water becomes clear. In a small pot bring rum and raisins to a full boil. If the rum flares up, remove it from the heat and allow the alcohol to burn off. Let raisins steep in rum for the duration.

In a large pot combine rice, milk, vanilla, salt, cinnamon, and the zest of 1 lemon. On low heat simmer the rice mixture. Do not allow the rice to come to a hard boil. Cook rice until tender, stirring occasionally. Set aside to cool for 10 minutes. Chill in the refrigerator for 30 minutes and serve.

The Isleños (Spanish word for islander) came from the Canary Islands off the coast of western Africa during the American Revolution. They were sent by King Juan Carlos III to protect Louisiana from the British. Most Isleños settled in St. Bernard Parish in Louisiana, some in Florida, San Antonio, Texas, Cuba, and Venezuela between 1731 and 1783. In Louisiana, Isleños were known for their cattle training, fishing, hunting, sugar cultivation, and farming skills. In the nineteenth century they worked on sugar plantations harvesting sugar and cypress.

The Isleños language, culture, and cuisine contributed greatly to the preservation of Spanish culture, language, and food in New Orleans. Samantha Perez stated in the book *The Isleños of Louisiana: On the Water's Edge* (2011), "The better world they hope for is one of full stomachs, laughter, barbecue, bare feet on burning wooden wharf, the closeness of family, the buzz of a flying cast net and, always, happiness. Every action in their daily lives is an unconscious fight to preserve their traditions in an ever changing world." In St. Bernard Parish, the Los Isleños Heritage and Cultural Society Museum continues to preserve Isleños culture, and every spring Los Isleños Fiesta Festival celebrates their food, language, and culture.

EDGAR M. SIERRA JIMENEZ

Edgar M. Sierra Jimenez (May 29, 1961, Medellin, Colombia) is a poet, photographer, and waiter at K-Paul's Louisiana Kitchen restaurant in the French Quarter. He moved to New Orleans in October of 1975 as a teenager with his three brothers and three sisters to join his father, who was working as a machinist at Avondale Shipyards. Since the 1990s, Edgar has worked as a waiter at many New Orleans restaurants such as Castillo's, Sante Fe, Brennan's, Broussard's, and Emeril's.

I was fifteen years old when I came to New Orleans from Colombia. I started working as a teenager in the restaurant industry early on. Growing up here in New Orleans gave me an understanding of the strong influence of not only Spain but Latin America, too, because so many people of Latin American origin were working in the kitchen where I worked. As I reflect on the history of cooks in New Orleans, you can't deny that black cooks made a major contribution to the cuisine [of] the city! Who do you think was doing the majority of the cooking back then? They were there introducing their culture and nuances into the same dishes that make New Orleans cuisine famous. You can also not deny that if today you have a lot of Latin Americans working in the kitchen their culinary influences are going to give a new twist to the food no matter how classic the recipe is. Growing up in Louisiana was beautiful but a learning experience, too, because I had to teach myself my own history. I had to read and research it. I was kind of amused after Katrina when I read headlines in the Times-Picayune *about the "Mexican invasion." There was a major paranoia that the Mexicans were going to take over and that the cultural identity of the city was going to be destroyed. New Orleans would become Nueva Orleans. I found that to be amusing when Latinos were always here. I love New Orleans because it reminds me of the school I went to in Colombia. I went to school with blacks, mestizos, and whites. It didn't matter! When I came as a teenager to New Orleans from Colombia I went to Beauregard High School, which is now called Thurgood Marshall. I was placed in a bilingual program with mostly Hondurans. Eighty percent of the school was African American and 20 percent were Latinos, mostly Hondurans. There was a sense of shame of being an immigrant and Hispanic at that time, so we clung to our dances, our music, and our food. It was only a matter of time before we would get acknowledged as fountains of culinary and musical cultural joy.*

Two places stand out in my memory of growing up in New Orleans, La Union Super Market and the Latin American Club. Back then all Latinos shopped at La Union Super Market on Carrollton, which is now in Kenner. The entire community was there. Then every week we would hang out at the Latin American Club uptown in the Garden District. You had the Hondurans, Nicaraguans, Salvadoreans, the Cubans; everybody was there. The food was where everybody kind of said there is no confusion of accents or arguments on the proper way to say things. The food was it and everybody was happy. You see, our foods are a pure reflection of who we are even if we start to lose the connection to our country. I remember the Cubans made delicious black beans and ropa vieja. Unbelievable! The Hondurans made yucca with chicharrónes and a cabbage salad that was so good. The Puerto Ricans made arroz con gandules and lechon that would just melt in your mouth. Back then you went to Latin American and you knew you were an outcast and you were just there to share what you have and where you were from. Today it is not like that. You can see Spanish words like empanada and jalapeño on the menu, and all of a sudden everyone loves Latin music and is dancing in the same club. So I guess being Spanish is no longer an embarrassment.

While Edgar was preparing his rendition of Bananas Foster at his home in the summer of 2009, he shared his boyhood memories and the day he made Bananas Foster for the first time.

Somebody told me once that New Orleans is like a handkerchief, small and dirty and you can put it in your pocket. Everyone knows each other or they know someone you know. When they have a funeral people will stop. It has that sense of community, a timeless flavor and a sense of the old world. It reminds me of Latin America. Sometimes when I go on a walk throughout the city it brings me back to my childhood in Colombia. I can smell some-body frying pork or garlic. That whiff just takes me back. I can't see myself living in Seattle. Not saying Seattle is bad, but I just like being connected to the past and my country. When I was a little boy my grandmother used to put ripe plantains with butter in the oven and add a little cinnamon and honey. Then when I was a young man living in New Orleans and I had to learn how to make Bananas Foster at Brennan's Restaurant it reminded me so much of my grandmother's plantain dessert. So no recipe is born in a void. Everything is very much connected. We will never know the whole story. But I will never forget the day I made Bananas Foster for the first time at Brennan's Restaurant. I put too much alcohol in the pan and the flame went so high. The chef came running out and asked me to please not set the restaurant on fire. He nearly had a heart attack. I got it right the next time!

During the 1930s through the 1950s, the United Fruit Company shipped from Central America a total of 65 million stems which contained billions of bananas. New Orleans's port was central to the United Fruit Company's trade operations in Central America. *The Great White Fleet*, United Fruit Company's steamship liner, ran ads monthly in *Lucero Latino* 1934, a New Orleans magazine for Latino elites living in New Orleans, inviting them to travel to northern cities, Central America, and the Caribbean. The steamship brought tons of bananas, cacao, and sugar froms Latin America to New Orleans's port. After World War II, the cartoon brand icon Chiquita was developed to market bananas for North American and European consumption. United Fruit Company's headquarters was located at 321 St. Charles Avenue.

Bananas Foster, a New Orleans classic dessert, was created in the 1950s by Chef Paul Blangé at the famous Brennan's Restaurant in New Orleans after his boss, Owen Brennan, challenged him to incorporate bananas into a new dish since New Orleans was flooded with bananas. The new culinary creation was named Bananas Foster after Brennan's friend Richard Foster, crime commissioner of New Orleans at that time. Edgar made Bananas Foster for me in his eclectic home in the summer of 2009; it is a dish that he makes almost daily for patrons at K-Paul's Louisiana Kitchen in the French Quarter. After devouring this classic dessert, I thought it would be a great idea to switch bananas with plantains. Edgar agreed and loved the idea! We made it together and it was beyond sinful.

Banano de Foster a lo Latino
Bananas Foster Latin Style

Makes about 3 servings: 10 minutes prep time, 20 minutes cooking time

Ingredients

4 ripe blackjack plantains (plantains should be turning black but still be somewhat firm)
½ cup of brown sugar
⅓ cup of unsalted butter
¼ cup of dark rum
¼ cup of banana liqueur
1 teaspoon of cinnamon powder
Good quality French vanilla ice cream

Preparation

Remove plantain peels and cut the plantains on a slant, about 1 inch in size.

Sauté the brown sugar and butter, constantly stirring until caramelized.

Add cinnamon and then the plantains. Add a little water so the plantains won't stick. When the plantains begin to soften and cook down, add the rum carefully. Tilt the pan over the fire slightly to ignite the rum. When the flame subsides, add the banana liqueur and serve over two scoops of vanilla ice cream.

Café brûlot is still served in many fine dining restaurants in New Orleans after a hearty meal. In the 1890s, Jules Alciatore invented what was then called Café Brûlot Diabolique. This coffee recipe ignited with brandy and spices. It was a treat for many New Orleanians and an entertaining scene of a waiter igniting coffee in a fancy chafing dish. During Prohibition, café brûlot was a great way to disguise alcohol intake. Edgar and I thought that café brûlot would be great with the classic Latino dessert flan. The richness of the flan and the exquisite taste of café brûlot gives a whole new meaning to flan.

Flan de Café Brûlot
Café Brûlot Flan

Makes about 4–5 servings: 30 minutes prep time, 2 hours cooking time

Ingredients

2 cups of coffee, preferably made with chicory

1 large orange peel

1 large lemon peel

10 whole cloves

2 cinnamon sticks

2 ounces of good brandy

4 ounces of good cognac

Café brûlot preparation

Light the burner under a chafing dish or pot. Cut the orange and lime peels so that the peels look like a long ribbon. Stick the cloves into the orange and lime peels. Add to the pot cinnamon sticks, brandy, and cognac. Pour in the coffee. With a fork, puncture both the orange and lime peels to hold firmly over the bowl. Ignite the alcohol and ladle the coffee mixture over the orange and lime peel. When the fire goes out remove orange and lime peels and the cinnamon sticks. Let cool.

Flan ingredients

½ cup of brown sugar

4 eggs, separated

1 14-ounce can of condensed milk

1 12-ounce can of evaporated milk

3 ounces of cream cheese

½ cup of Nestle Table Cream/media crema (sold in Latin
    grocery stores)
A dash of salt

Flan preparation

Preheat oven to 350 degrees. In a pan, combine brown sugar
and ⅓ cup of café brûlot. Boil on low medium heat rapidly
until it becomes a thick sauce. Pour the brûlot mixture into
the bottom of a medium-sized glass or ceramic ovenproof
dish. Move brûlot mixture around until the bottom of the dish
is coated. Let cool.

In a food processor or blender, mix eggs, milks, cream
cheese, and table cream and then add vanilla and salt. Pour
into pan.

Place dish in large roasting pan or deep pan. Boil hot water
and pour it into the roasting pan until the hot water is halfway
filled in the pan. Bake flan in water bath for 1 hour. Remove
ceramic or glass dish from the water bath. Let cool, cover,
then chill overnight or for 4 hours at least.

Remove flan from the refrigerator. Take a larger-sized plate
to put on top of the flan dish and then rapidly and firmly flip
the flan so that the flan lands on the plate.

Brûlot sauce

½ cup of brown sugar
⅓ cup of café brûlot

Sauté brown sugar and café brûlot until it caramelizes and the
sauce thickens. Cool for 5 minutes and pour over flan.

Cut the flan into pie wedges and serve.

CHEF ADOLFO GARCIA

Chef Adolfo Garcia (April 26, 1961, New Orleans, Louisiana) was born to two loving Panamanian parents and grew up in Metairie, Louisiana, a suburb of New Orleans, during the 1970s. As a teenager, he washed dishes for Pancho's Mexican restaurant in Metairie. Garcia recognized his passion for the culinary arts and moved to New York, where he graduated from the prestigious Culinary Institute of America. After graduation, he experienced other cities as a chef but was determined to return to New Orleans to cook the food that he grew up eating, Latino and New Orleans cuisine. Today, Chef Garcia is the owner of Rio Mar, A Mano, and La Boca in the New Orleans Warehouse District. He has many accolades, such as Top 8 Latino Chefs in the Country, *Hispanic Magazine,* and James Beard 2010 semifinalist for Best Chef of the South.

The first person to encourage me was Paul Prudhomme. Paul Prudhomme cooks Cajun food. Today Cajun food is mainstream, but when I was a young man growing up in New Orleans no one was cooking Cajun food in New Orleans. People cooked Creole food. We never ate boudin, andouille, or gumbo in New Orleans like they make in the country. Prudhomme came as a young man to New Orleans in the 1970s cooking Creole food, a cuisine he did not grow up eating. Brennan helped him become the chef he is at Commander's Palace. After leaving Commander's Palace he opened his restaurant and served real Cajun food. Before I decided to go to culinary school I approached him and told him what I wanted to do, and he encouraged me and told me to go school and be the best I could be. He inspired me as a cook and so did chefs like Susan Spicer and John Neal. They weren't cooking trout meunière amandine, shrimp remoulade, or shrimp Creole. They were cooking what they wanted to cook so they kind of broke the mode of New Orleans Creole. You could take any Creole restaurant at the time and they all had the same menu. I would come home from culinary school in New York and I would eat at Susan Spicer's place and John Neal's and I said, wow! I think I can come home now because I don't have to cook Creole food. I love Creole food, but I don't have to cook it. I could cook my food and New Orleanians would still accept it. From the day I opened my first restaurant, Criollo (now closed), I wanted to serve food that is a reflection of my culture and experiences. That is what makes our restaurant unique. There are restaurants in New Orleans that serve Creole food and there isn't one Creole in the entire restaurant. So a lot of times when there are people like Donald Link who actually come from bayou country you know his food comes from his heart, and you know it is going to be so much better than someone who learned it out of a book. How many people come to New Orleans to eat Latin food? Probably not that many but that wasn't my concern. I just wanted to serve the best food I could and I believed in the saying "build it and they will come." We are successful because we cook from the heart and we cook true to what we believe in. It's historically correct and my food is always based in tradition. What we cook in Rio Mar is inspired by me being born in New Orleans and all the great products we have here in the Gulf of Mexico, the flavors I tasted when I was younger, and also my Latin upbringing is essential to what we do. Also, my experiences cooking in New York and Spain more than anything were the big driving forces for everything we do. To me, New Orleans is a better opportunity than Miami and New York because we don't have blinders on saying this is what food is. Try changing a Cuban sandwich in Miami. Never! Here you can reinterpret and make Latino food what you want.

Chicharrón de Corvina Negra, Patacones con Cangrejo y Salsa de Aguacate
Louisiana Drum with Crabmeat, Plantains, and Avocado Remoulade

Makes about 2 servings: 30 minutes prep time, 25 minutes cooking time

Ingredients

1 large green plantain, peeled and sliced

¼ cup of cilantro, chopped

2 small avocados

1 red onion, diced

2 teaspoons of capers

1 stalk of celery, chopped

1 hard-boiled egg

1 green onion, chopped

2 teaspoons of mayonnaise

1 teaspoon of Creole mustard

1 lime, juiced

3 dashes of Tabasco sauce

4 teaspoons of olive oil

Salt and pepper

2 8-ounce filets of black drum, skin on, or redfish

6 ounces jumbo lump crabmeat (pick meat free of shell, season and dress with a splash of olive oil, and season to taste)

Preparation

Fry plantain until light golden brown in 275 degrees peanut oil or canola oil. Let plaintains cool. Smash plantains with the back of a pan or *tostonera* (plantain smasher). Reserve. Mix crabmeat, cilantro, and salt and pepper. Reserve. In a food processor, mix avocados, ½ of a small red onion, capers, celery, 1 hard-boiled egg, green onion, mayonnaise, Creole mustard, squeezed lime juice, Tabasco sauce, olive oil, and salt and pepper. Pulse and reserve.

Season fish with salt and pepper. In a hot oiled pan, sauté fish skin side down till crisp and almost fully cooked on the skin side. Turn over 30 seconds until done. Fry the patacones (plantains) and season liberally with salt. Assemble dish by putting avocado remoulade on plate, then fish on top. Put patacones on the fish, top with crabmeat mixture, and garnish with cilantro.

For most of the nineteenth century and a large part of the twentieth century, Latinos lived in Orleans Parish. When Jefferson Parish swamplands were drained in the 1950s and a levee system was built, affordable homes, safer neighborhoods, and better schools enticed many middle- and upper-class Latino families to leave the city. From 1970 to 2000 Orleans Parish lost 11 percent of its Latino population and Jefferson Parish gained 15 percent. However, before Hurricane Katrina, many Latinos came back to the city to do their grocery shopping at La Union Super Market or eat in Latino restaurants. After Katrina many restaurants folded and La Union Super Market moved out to Kenner. Today, throughout Jefferson Parish, the Latino population continues to grow and so does the need to feed the Latin American palate.

MARGARITA SANCHEZ GARCIA

Margarita Sanchez Garcia (March 23, 1954, El Seibo, Dominican Republic) is an accountant for Rio Mar, A Mano, and La Boca, a stay-at-home mom, a volunteer cook for orphans, and the wife of Chef Adolfo Garcia. Margarita moved to New York when she was twenty years old, after her father died, to help her mother care for Margarita's eight siblings.

My mother had to feed us so she moved to New York to work in a factory. All of us were scattered when my mother left, living with family and one of us living in an orphanage. I was one of the last ones to move and I hated New York. I lived in Queens in Corona Heights but eventually I learned English and started to enjoy New York. I had three jobs when I met my husband, Adolfo. I was always busy and I traveled a lot.

Chef Adolfo Garcia was going to be a lawyer and was close to graduating from law school when he decided to move to New York to study culinary arts. Margarita met her husband at a salsa club in New York while he was studying at the Culinary Institute of America.

When I met Adolfo he told me that if we were to get married I would have to move to New Orleans. I didn't know that much about New Orleans, but he talked about it all the time. We got married and had our son in New York. I remember that day because it was a snowstorm in New York. Adolfo called an ambulance and said, "Please come, my wife is in labor! I'm from New Orleans, I don't know how to drive in the snow." (She laughs infectiously.) When we finally moved to New Orleans, people were so friendly. They are very affectionate here. I remember when I saw a car accident everyone stopped to see if they could help. That would have never happened in New York. Everyone was smiling and Adolfo would say, "Baby, this is not New York." When I got here people would ask me, "Margarita, are you on amphetamines?" Because I was always doing something but that is how you are when you live in New York. It took me a while to get used to life out here. I say they are the

American Spanish people. You go to the grocery store and the cashier talks to you and wants to hold conversations with you. If that type of cashier was in New York people would want to shoot her. When we first moved here the first thing Adolfo did was take me to eat a po'boy and I loved it! I love my husband's food, but he doesn't cook in my house. I cook.

Margarita and Adolfo still dance salsa. Each night after many hours at the restaurant, they pop open a bottle of wine, eat a hearty meal, and dance salsa until the sun rises.
(Interview was translated from Spanish.)

Moro de Gandules con Carne de Tasso
Rice with Pigeon Peas and Tasso

Makes about 6 servings: 15 minutes prep time,
30 minutes cooking time

Ingredients
½ of a green bell pepper, diced
½ of a red onion, diced
2 cloves of garlic
¼ cup of tasso meat, diced
1 chicken bouillon cube
¼ cup of cilantro
1 15-ounce can of pigeon peas/gandules
1 large tablespoon of tomato paste
1 tablespoon of vinegar
1½ cups of rice

Preparation
In a mortar, mash garlic, cilantro, salt, pepper, and oregano with a pestle. Set aside. To make the *sofrito*, heat 2 tablespoons of olive oil and sauté onion, bell pepper, garlic mixture, and tasso for 5 minutes until the onions are translucent. Add tomato paste and the bouillon cube. Add the pigeon peas and stir. Add vinegar and then add water and rice. (Hint: for every cup of rice you add 1½ cups of water.) Cover and boil on low medium heat for 20 to 30 minutes until rice is fully cooked. Garnish with cilantro.

Moro de gandules is a Dominican rice and bean dish similar to Puerto Rico's arroz con gandules and Jamaican rice and peas. Rice and beans are eaten daily throughout Latin America and the Caribbean. The cultivation of rice in Latin America and Louisiana was brought by West African slaves, and beans were native to the Americas. However, gandules, or pigeon peas, were cultivated in Africa thousands of years ago and were probably brought to the Americas during the slave trade. The Spanish love for pork was usually incorporated into rice and beans for flavor. Margarita added tasso meat, a peppery cured Cajun ham, to give moro de gandules a new flavor.

EXECUTIVE CHEF JACK MARTINEZ

Executive Chef Jack Martinez (Querétaro, México) says that his great-great-grandparents lived in New Orleans during the 1800s and returned to México during political unrest in New Orleans. Mexican migrants to Louisiana fled to México, Haiti, and France. In 1860 the *New Orleans Daily Delta* newspaper ran an article discussing the exodus to México. As fate would have it, in the 1980s, Martinez migrated from México as a young man and moved to Houston, Texas, where he worked in restaurants from the bottom up. He then moved to New Orleans after closing his restaurant for personal reasons. Martinez was hired as executive chef at Dickie Brennan's Steakhouse in the famous French Quarter. Chef Martinez, with twenty-five years of experience cooking Italian, Creole, French, and Spanish dishes, helped to make Dickie Brennan's Steakhouse one of the top steakhouses in America, named by the

Wall Street Journal. Chef Martinez's Crab Cakes with Salsa Verde are a favorite at Dickie Brennan's Steakhouse. In this dish he uses traditional Mexican cooking methods taught to him by his mother.

I love this city! When I came here I brought my passion for food and the Mexican tradition of cooking that I was taught by my mother. I am very proud that during my time as executive chef at Dickie Brennan's Steakhouse it was voted as one of the top steakhouses in America in a seafood-run town. I have cooked for so many just being here and I have traveled all over representing New Orleans and my style of cooking. New Orleans has become my home. I guess it always has been home for my family since my great-great-grandparents lived here long ago. I just came back to continue our tradition of good food in a great city. (Interview was translated from Spanish.)

Torta de Cangrejo con Salsa Verde
Crab Cakes with Green Salsa

Makes about 3 servings: 20 minutes prep time,
10 minutes cooking time

Ingredients

4 roasted garlic cloves

2 tomatillos (small green tomatoes)

1 jalapeño

1 ounce of cilantro, chopped

1 ripe avocado, diced

2 limes

1 pound of jumbo crabmeat

1 cup of mayonnaise

½ squeezed lemon

1 tablespoon of unsalted butter

Salsa verde preparation

On a flat cast-iron skillet roast 4 garlic cloves with peels, 2 skin-removed tomatillos, and 1 jalapeño until charred. In a blender mix the 2 peeled garlic cloves, 2 tomatillos, and 1 jalapeño. In a mixing bowl, fold in avocado and cilantro. Squeeze 1 lime and stir. Set aside.

Crab cake preparation

Discard any loose crab shells in the crabmeat. Gently fold mayonnaise and 2 roasted minced garlic cloves into crabmeat. Squeeze ½ of a lemon over the crab mixture. Add salt and pepper, then place crab mixture in a ring mold.

Sauté in unsalted butter on both sides with a spatula until golden brown. Serve with salsa verde.

ROMAN CASTILLO

Roman Castillo (October 18, 1984, New Orleans, Louisiana) grew up in the French Quarter during the 1980s. His father, Carlos Zwinglio Castillo, from Sabinas, México, taught Roman how to cook from an early age at the once-family-owned restaurant, Castillo's, in the French Quarter. Roman's first memories are of his father teaching him how to make eggs and a roux. Castillo Sr. settled in New Orleans after many years of working as a merchant marine. He opened Castillo's restaurant with his wife, Maria Ines Castillo, from Copán, Honduras. Castillo Sr. made homemade chorizo daily and traveled yearly to the Yucatán Peninsula to pick a variety of fresh chilies for his restaurant. Castillo's Mexican restaurant was open for thirty-six years until it closed in 2000. Roman, reminiscing about his childhood, said that the first thing that most Latinos try when moving to the South is grits, and in this recipe he wanted to incorporate his own heritage and his love for New Orleans. "I chose my recipe because Mexican and Cajun are very similar. They both rely on strong flavors and slow cooking methods, and the flavors are robust. I didn't eat grits until I went to my friend's house. They were Cajun. At home, we ate a lot of eggs and rice for breakfast or brunch with tomatoes and cumin in it, but today I eat grits as much as I do my dad's food."

The first time I noticed that I grew up differently was when I was in school at St. Dominic in New Orleans. Most of my classmates lived in New Orleans suburbs but I grew up in the French Quarter where there weren't many kids. So I didn't have many friends except for adults who worked in the French Quarter or for my father. My father ran the restaurant downstairs and we lived on the second floor. We rented rooms to the cook and the dishwasher on the third and fourth floors. It was all of us in one building. We were all Latino. I remember waking up in the morning and being able to go downstairs into a fully functioning restaurant, and I would go in the kitchen to make whatever I wanted before the restaurant opened. Sometimes my dad would be in the kitchen with me teaching me how to make simple things like a roux, scrambled eggs, enchiladas, and nachos. He would give me a little piece of tortilla to try the roux.

My dad's food was unlike any Mexican food in the state of Louisiana. It was way less Tex-Mex but rather traditional Mexican in comparison to many restaurants across the U.S. that are more Tex-Mex, in my opinion. He used really authentic ingredients. When we had the restaurant, he would fly into the Yucatán Peninsula to Oaxaca to buy bags of spices to bring back for the restaurant. Everything that was being used in the restaurant came from México.

He would make his sauces every day the traditional Mexican way. He was a legend before his time. When he moved here it was a really busy port. He enjoyed the French Quarter and what he called "the action." We were located at 620 Conti. It is a bar now. What I remember from my childhood is that the building was totally haunted. It is a really old building. It used to be a fencing school in the 1800s. Sometimes my parents would be downstairs and I would be on the second floor watching TV and I would hear people walking on the floor above me but no one was up there. My mom reported the same things and she would go up there and no one was there. Various times we would feel like someone was standing over our bed but no one was there. There was a stairwell that connected the floors. My cousin and I would play there and one time we heard someone or something say, "Shhhhhhh." We bolted and got out of there.

The book *Lost Restaurants of New Orleans* by Peggy Scott Laborde and Tom Fitzmorris (2011) explains that Mexican food was not commonplace in New Orleans, yet Carlos Castillo was known for his authentic Mexican cuisine. Each dish was prepared with great skill and precision. Castillo's restaurant was famous for its caldo xochil, mole poblano, and chilmole de puerco. "Owner Carlos Castillo was a unique character . . . He could talk for a long time on the history of Mexico and its cuisine and give you a full dogma about how authentic Mexican food needed to be cooked . . . If Castillo's were still around, even with the same menu it would still be on the cutting edge by New Orleans standards." In 2011, Roman Castillo graduated from Nicholls State University with a degree in culinary arts. Today he cares for both his ailing parents and works at night as a chef at Zea's restaurant on the West Bank. He dreams of the day when he can reopen his father's restaurant.

New Orleans is a culinary hub. I remember eating as a kid a lot of Italian and Creole food, but now there are a lot of contemporary influences thanks to John Besh, Paul Prudhomme, and John Folse. These chefs pushed exponentially into more contemporary food. They paved the path for all of us. I want to cook my dad's food and reopen the restaurant. My mom is my book of recipes; she knows all of it by heart. I know a lot of his recipes through her. What keeps me in New Orleans? My desire to reopen our family restaurant and that I have an emotional attachment to the New Orleans Saints since I was a kid.

To me, the real definition of Creole food is an amalgamation of all nations. If you look at ethnic restaurants, go to the West Bank and you will see a lot of Vietnamese and Central America food. Amazing food! Creole food continuously defines and establishes itself through the population and how different flavors and ethnicities meld into a new food. My food is in there. It's like a dollar in the basket—you can take a lot of approaches from different nations and put it together. For example, the dish I did for this book. The chorizo is Mexican with shrimp and grits, which is traditionally southern. Then the parsley sauce uses a French technique. I was classically trained in French cuisine from culinary school, but I know my parents' food. I can combine and improve on Mexican dishes with French techniques and French dishes with Mexican techniques. I just stand waiting for my opportunity to show people my food. I know my dad wants me to open up again and that is how I will continue with his legacy. I like it that Latino chefs tend to hold on to their traditions tightly; it is really admirable. They stick to their roots. But I embrace both cultures. It allows me to be the most creative when I have more ideas to work with. It is better to expose yourself to more food.

Maiz de Maque Choux con Camarones Asada con Chorizo y una Torta de Maiz Molido
Corn Maque Choux with Sauteed Shrimp and Chorizo with Grit Cake

Makes about 5 servings: 30 minutes prep time,
1 hour cooking time

Ingredients

2 cups of stone-ground grits

4 tablespoons of unsalted butter for grits

½ pound of Spanish chorizo or Mexican chorizo

4 or 5 ears of fresh corn (with a sharp knife remove kernels and pass knife over the ear to collect corn milk; yields 2 cups of fresh corn; reserve corn milk in a bowl)

1 each small green, red, and yellow bell peppers, diced

2 garlic cloves, diced

1 small white onion, finely minced

1 teaspoon of K-Paul's Vegetable Magic

1 teaspoon of smoked paprika

1 teaspoon of chili powder

1 tablespoon of honey

A pinch of cayenne pepper

1½ pounds of fresh jumbo shrimp, peeled, with tails on (preferably Gulf Coast shrimp)

1 teaspoon of K-Paul's Seafood Magic

1 cup of shrimp stock

4 garlic cloves, finely chopped

1 cup of quality white wine

¼ cup of fresh parsley, chopped

Shrimp stock preparation

Boil 20 shrimp shells, 20 shrimp heads, the white heads of green onions, garlic peels, ends of jalapeños, and ends of bell peppers. Boil for 20 to 30 minutes, strain, and reserve liquid.

Grit cake preparation

Boil 4 cups of water and add 1 cup of stone-ground grits. Whisk constantly until semithick. Add 3 tablespoons of unsalted butter and salt and pepper. Pour grits into a cake ramekin. Freeze for 10 to 15 minutes and then refrigerate for 30 minutes. Remove grit cake from the refrigerator and cut into small squares and then a triangle. Set triangle grit cake with the pointy edge on the plate.

Corn maque choux and chorizo preparation

Sauté chorizo for 5 minutes. Drain oil and set aside in a bowl. In the same pan sauté half of the diced onions and garlic until onions are translucent. Add chorizo. Sauté in the same pan 1 tablespoon of unsalted butter, corn milk, olive oil, 2 cups of fresh corn, peppers, the other half of the diced garlic and onions. Season with K-Paul's Vegetable Magic, smoked paprika, and chili powder. Cook for an additional 10 minutes. Add 1 tablespoon of honey and cayenne pepper. Set aside.

Shrimp preparation

Remove shells from shrimp but leave the tails on. Mix shrimp with K-Paul's Seafood Magic. Sauté 1 stick of salted butter until butter turns to a caramel color. Do not overcook! Sear on both sides for 2 minutes. Remove shrimp and deglaze the pan with 1 teaspoon of unsalted butter, 1 cup of shrimp stock, and 1 cup of wine, then reintroduce shrimp to the pan. Cook shrimp until they turn pink, about 3 minutes on low-medium heat. Reserve shrimp and space them on a plate so they don't cook each other. Warm grit cake in the microwave for 1 minute covering it with a paper towel. Remove grit cake from the microwave and plate. With a large spoon sprinkle chorizo mixture over the grit cake. Place 3 jumbo shrimps on the plate. Use a spoon to pour butter-wine mixture over the cake. Garnish with fresh chopped parsley and serve.

Maque choux is traditionally a Cajun dish with Native American influences. The traditional dish includes bacon grease, green bell peppers, corn, tomatoes, onions, and sometimes garlic and celery and historically was served on holidays, Sundays, and birthdays.

KID CHEF ELIANA

Kid Chef Eliana (June 15, 2000, New Orleans, Louisiana) had, by the time she was eleven years old, written two cookbooks, *Eliana Cooks! Recipes for Creative Kids* (2010) and *Cool Kids Cook: Louisiana* (2012). Kid Chef Eliana was greatly influenced by her Cuban grandfather, who passed down his family recipes and wisdom to his beloved granddaughter. Eliana's passion for cooking is attributed to her diverse family members: Cajun, Cuban, Honduran, Filipino, and Spanish. She has a gumbo of family recipes, and Kid Chef Eliana's sole mission is to teach kids that cooking is fun!

He always made Cuban sandwiches, tostones (fried plantains), and black beans, but he never shared his recipes with all of us, just me. He taught me how to make a Cuban sandwich with mojo sauce. But I make it with French bread and Creole mustard. He also taught me how to make con gris, which is black beans and rice mixed together. My grandfather was always in the kitchen. He kept the dishes clean. He would not let them pile up. As soon as you were done you *had to wash them immediately. He died when I was eight.*

My Honduran abuela always makes baleada (tortilla filled with refried beans, Honduran cream, and cheese). She taught me how to make tostones, fritters, and Johnny cakes. She mixes in food from New Orleans and food from Guanaja, Honduras. She is very tied to her Honduran roots. She makes a good gumbo too.

Everyone has a specialty in our family. For Thanksgiving we usually have three Cajun fried turkeys, my nana's lumpia (fried spring roll), and garlic fried rice from the Philippines, Cuban mojo pork, my Cajun pastalaya, which is just jambalaya but with pasta, my mom's Asian green beans, sweet potato pie, and Cajun boiled red potatoes.

Eliana commented on her culinary philosophy: *"I want everyone to cook and to cook fresh because it is healthy and it tastes a lot better than something in a jar and canned. Food brings families together. You sit at the dinner table and talk. I always tell kids, don't eat the same things all of the time. Try everything!*

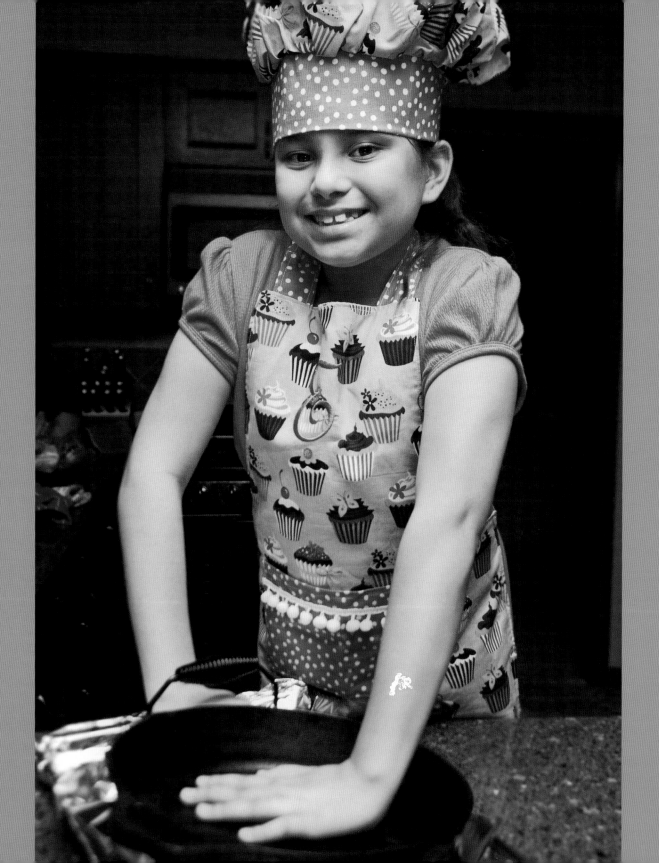

Sandwich Cubano a lo Cajun
Cajun Cuban Sandwich

Makes about 2 sandwiches: 30 minutes prep time,
4 hours cooking time

Ingredients:

3-pound pork tenderloin

1 bottle of Goya Mojo Criollo marinade

4 cloves of garlic

1 loaf of French bread

Swiss cheese

Deli ham

Creole mustard

Pickle slices

Pork preparation

In a large roasting pan, puncture pork tenderloin with a fork
and pour mojo marinade over the pork and bury the garlic
in the holes. Cover and marinate overnight in the refrigerator. Preheat oven to 375 degrees. Cover and roast the pork
for 3 hours. Let pork cool for 30 minutes and then shred it
with a fork.

Sandwich preparation

Spread Creole mustard lightly over French bread. Add a gen-
erous amount of pork. Add a slice of Swiss cheese and then
a few slices of deli ham. Top with sliced pickles and press
the sandwich in a panini press or place the sandwich on a
baking sheet, cover with aluminum foil, and place a heavy
cast-iron skillet on top of the sandwich. Press down. Bake
in the oven for 5–7 minutes until the bread is crisp and the
cheese is melted.

The Cuban sandwich, similar to the New
Orleans po'boy, was created for the working
class. Although the famous ham sandwich was
originally created in Cuba in the early part of the
twentieth century and is known for its bread and
mojo-flavored roasted pork, other ingredients
have been added by immigrants to Ybor City,
Florida, such as glazed ham from Spain and salami
from Italy. Ybor City and New Orleans were home
to many cigar factories and political exiles during
the Spanish-American War and the Cuban revolution. Between the 1950s and 1980s, Cuban sandwiches were predominately sold on Magazine
Street in New Orleans, where Cubans migrated
during that period. Today, Cuban sandwiches are
sold in Jefferson Parish grocery stores such as La
Union Super Market and Norma's Sweets Bakery.
At John Besh's Lüke restaurant in New Orleans,
Cochon de Lait Pressed Sandwich bears a striking
similarity to the famous Cuban sandwich.

NANCY GONSALVES

Nancy Gonsalves (Monterrey, México) moved to New Orleans in 1996 with her husband and two daughters. Gonsalves sells tamales, jars of fresh salsa, and vegetables at Gretna's farmers' market every weekend. Her oldest daughter helps her sell on Saturdays and helps her plant okra to be sold at the market. Gonsalves used to help her *comadre* (godmother) sell tamales until she learned from her how to make tamales New Orleans style.

New Orleans–style tamales are different from the tamales I grew up eating in México, but they are still good and my customers always come back. Back home we use more spices and our tamales have less masa (dough) than a lot of tamales I've tried since I've been here. There are so many ways to make tamales, and what part of México you are from determines what kind of tamale you eat. I can't say that I don't miss home and my food, but this is my home now. At the market, I do my best to make sure that I sell what people need and what they like—my tamales, okra that I pick from a friend's farm, fresh salsa, and homemade tortilla chips. I don't think my customers are ready for my tamales from my country. They like New Orleans–style tamales.

(Interview was translated from Spanish.)

Tamales a lo Nueva Orleans
New Orleans–Style Tamales

Hint: Purchase a large pot made especially for tamales called a *tamalera*. It makes the tamale-making process so much simpler. Most Hispanic grocery stores sell them.

Makes about 15 servings: 1 hour prep time, 30 minutes cooking time

Ingredients
16-ounce bag of *guajillo* peppers

2 bay leaves

2 cloves of garlic

1 tablespoon of cumin

1 small yellow onion

1 teaspoon of white vinegar

2 yellow onions, diced

3 pounds of ground beef

3 pouinds of ground pork

⅓ cup of Cajun seasoning

⅓ cup of Goya Adobo seasoning or chicken flavor
   bouillon

1 litre of chicken broth

1 cup of Manteca or lard

2.4 pounds of Maseca Instant Corn Masa Mix

2 teaspoons of baking powder

16-ounce package of corn tamale husks (sold at
   Hispanic grocery stores)

Tamale ties, string, or strip of husk

8 cups of water or more

***Guajillo* sauce and meat preparation**

In a pot of boiling water boil *guajillo* peppers with 2 bay
leaves until peppers are semisoft. Strain and reserve liquid
and peppers. Discard bay leaves. Remove stems from the
peppers. Blend all peppers with 4 cups of reserved liquid,
1 garlic clove, 1 teaspoon of cumin, 1 small yellow onion,
2 teaspoons of salt, and 1 teaspoon of white vinegar.
Refrigerate sauce for 1 hour or overnight for better taste
and consistency.

Mix ground beef and ground pork in a large bowl with
Cajun and Adobo seasonings. Chop 2 medium-sized onions
finely. Sauté onions and add meat mixture. Cook until done.
Strain meat with a colander to remove any excess oil. In a
large bowl add 2 cups of *guajillo* sauce (reserve the rest of
the sauce in the refrigerator), 1 cup at a time, and cover and
reserve meat in the refrigerator.

New Orleans has had a tradition of tamale-making since the late eighteenth century when Mexicans were brought to New Orleans by the Spanish. Tamales became so popular in New Orleans that the jazz cornetist Freddie Keppard sang a song dedicated to Mexicans in New Orleans called "Here Comes the Hot Tamale Man." Tamales continue to be a favorite staple in New Orleans. Manuel's Hot Tamales, founded in 1932, was a favorite for New Orleanians. Many people have fond memories of eating Manuel's hot tamales. Manuel Hernandez, born in Mexico City in 1894, the originator of Manuel's Hot Tamales, was a former musician turned tamale man who became a culinary legend in New Orleans. For nearly thirty years, Hernandez sold the cornmeal, greasy beef tamales every day from his pushcart until the late 1950s when the family opened a factory and restaurant on Carrollton Avenue. Unfortunately, the family-owned business was destroyed by Katrina and has yet to reopen. However, New Orleans–style tamales continue to be found throughout the parishes and are still a popular late-night street food.

Making the masa

Combine four cups of masa mix with 2 teaspoons of baking powder. Season lightly with Cajun seasoning and Adobo. Mix together. Now slowly pour in three cups of chicken broth (or water) and mix with a spatula or in a large food processor. Add 1 cup of Manteca into the masa dough and mix thoroughly.

Tamale preparation

Let tamale shells soak in boiling hot water for 2 hours in a *tamalera* or large pot. Tamale husks should be soft. Set aside. With a spatula, spoon masa mix and then a little of the meat mixture into tamale shells, making sure that the filling is far away from the edges. Tie tamales with tamale ties and roll with aluminum foil. Boil tamales for 45 minutes. Serve immediately or freeze for up to 3 weeks. Serve with *guajillo* sauce spooned over the tamales.

CARLOS HERNANDEZ

Carlos Hernandez (August 9, 1940, San Salvador, El Salvador) moved to New Orleans with his mother and siblings when he was a small boy. They resided in the Iberville projects, and he went to St. Joseph Catholic School on Tulane Avenue. In 1967, the New Orleans Saints football team was founded, and Carlos worked as part of the cleaning crew for the first Saints game. In 1969, Carlos was drafted and served in Vietnam. Because he had grown up in the Iberville projects during segregation, spoke limited English, served in Vietnam, and saw the first Saints game, the 2010 Saints Super Bowl victory felt like a personal victory to him.

I remember growing up in the Iberville projects. My mother worked so hard to send us to Catholic school and to make life better for us. I remember not knowing how to speak English as a child. Some kids at school who I thought were my friends told me to say a bad word in English to one of the nuns. I thought I was saying something kind and learning a new word in English. You should have seen the nun's face when I told her that ugly word. After

that, I spent every day studying the English dictionary until I learned how to speak English. Before I went to Vietnam in '69, I was part of a cleaning crew for the first Saints game. I remember seeing that first game. It was electrifying! When I was finally drafted to Vietnam, I spent my nights writing letters to my wife and remembering New Orleans.

Today, Carlos cooks and invites family and friends to enjoy his annual crawfish boil parties and to honor his mother's vision.

Forty-nine years in New Orleans and we're eating like everyone else. Crawfish is a Hernandez tradition. We love it! Our friends come over to watch the Saints games and we make huge pots of crawfish. Of course my wife makes tacos and chicharrónes (pork cracklins') on the side. But every time I see a Saints game I can't help but remember my mother and how far we have come. Every one of us has graduated from school. My family is doing well. I have a great life in New Orleans, and I know the Saints will win the Super Bowl! Seeing them win is like knowing that my mother won for

all of her hard work and sacrifice. My mother had a vision for all of us: a better life and a good education. I think she would be proud.
(Interview, November 2009, before the New Orleans Saints won the Super Bowl in February 2010.)

Langostina de Carlos
Carlos's Crawfish

Makes about 20 servings: 30 minutes prep time, 45 minutes cooking time

Ingredients

36 pounds of live crawfish

12 yellow onions, cut into pieces

1 bunch of celery, cut into pieces

3 heads of garlic, peeled

6 or 8 bay leaves

10 cut yellow lemons

1 container of crab boil (73 ounces); use about 55 ounces

1 pound of potatoes, cut into large chunks

6 links of sausage, cut into large chunks

1 big bag of small corn ears

Liquid boil, 16 ounces; use ⅔ of the bottle

Preparation

Using an 80-quart pot with steamer basket and propane burner, fill the pot with about 60 quarts of water. Let water come to a boil. Add 55 ounces of crab boil, ⅔ of liquid boil, bay leaves, celery, garlic, and onions. Cook for 5 minutes. Add potatoes and sausage. Cook for 15 minutes. Wash crawfish 3 times before adding to the pot. Add corn. Cover and cook for another 25 minutes. Turn the flame off and let the crawfish cool for 10 to 15 minutes. Serve with Corona or Abita beer and tacos.

Although south Louisiana newspapers in 1870 reported seeing "crawfish parties," the Breaux Bridge Crawfish Festival, started in 1959, popularized the peeling and boiling of crawfish in large pots for massive consumption. However, crawfish boils didn't gain popularity in the rest of Louisiana until the 1980s during the height of Cajun cuisine, in large part due to Chef Paul Prud-homme's notoriety and his introduction of Cajun cuisine to New Orleans and the world. Although crawfish boils are not part of Latin American cuisine, many Latinos in Louisiana have included crawfish boils as part of their family gatherings during soccer games, Saints games, and cook-outs. A dear friend of mine from the Dominican Republic invited me to a *fais-do-do* (a Cajun cook-out and dance) in the summer of 2010. He and his fellow Latino co-workers worked side by side for months at a time on the Gulf of México with their Cajun brethren. At the *fais-do-do* it was interesting to see my friend's Latino co-workers eat crawfish for the first time and enjoy the hospitality of their new Cajun friends.

ALEXEY MARTI

Alexey Marti (December 9, 1975, Havana, Cuba) migrated to New Orleans from Cuba in 2008. An accomplished composer and percussionist, he played with Irvin Mayfield, Los Hombres Calientes, Louisiana Philharmonic, Regeneration, and other New Orleans artists. Marti currently has his own band called Urban Minds. On his life in New Orleans he had this to say:

Men cook in Cuba the same as in New Orleans. They love sports like we do; they love the Saints like we love baseball. We are the same roots from the same plant, just in different places. They eat a lot of rice like we do, but in Cuba we use more of a variety of beans to cook with rice.

One time we had a house party for musicians and I made a huge meal Cuban style and they made New Orleans food. Mine was the first to go, maybe because they never tried my food before. Nothing is better than the other because our connection runs so deep: New Orleans, Cuba, and Brazil. I am learning this city. I am incorporating my music, who I am, and what they play here. (Interview was translated from Spanish.)

Garbanzos Fritos con Langostina
Fried Chickpeas with Crawfish

Makes about 1–2 servings: overnight and 30 minutes prep time, 45 minutes cooking time

Ingredients

2 cups of dry garbanzo beans

1 ham hock

2 bay leaves

2 tablespoons of olive oil

5 slices of good bacon, diced

¼ cup of Spanish chorizo or smoked sausage, sliced

4 garlic cloves, minced

1 teaspoon each of salt and ground black pepper

1 teaspoon each of thyme and oregano

1 teaspoon of ground cumin

3 ounces of thawed crawfish tails

1 lime

¼ cup of fresh cilantro, chopped

Preparation

Put 2 cups of dry garbanzo beans in a large bowl. Cover with water to the top and add a teaspoon of salt. Refrigerate

overnight. In a large stock pot pour refrigerated garbanzos, 1 ham hock; add water from the faucet to half of the pot, put in 2 bay leaves, and boil garbanzos for approximately 2 hours. Add water if necessary when it evaporates. Once the garbanzos become soft, drain in a colander but reserve ⅓ cup of the liquid. In a skillet, sauté bacon and chorizo at low-medium heat. Add minced garlic. Do not burn garlic. Add seasoning—salt, ground black pepper, thyme, oregano, and cumin. Add chickpeas. Cover and simmer at a low heat for 10 minutes. Add crawfish tails and simmer for another 5 minutes. Serve with cut limes and garnish with chopped cilantro.

Music and food are integral to the culture of both New Orleans and Latin America. Many songs were written in Latin America and New Orleans throughout the twentieth century that used food as the main subject or as a metaphor—songs like *"Sopa de Caracol"* by Banda Blanca, *"El Negro esta Cocinando"* by Los Van Van, *"Machucalo"* by Toño Rosario, *"A lo Cubano"* by Orishas, *"Arroz con Habichuela"* by El Gran Combo de Puerto Rico, "Here Comes the Hot Tamale Man" by Freddie Keppard, "Jambalaya" by Fats Domino, "Crawfish" by Elvis Presley, and "African Gumbo" by James Booker.

According to the book *Up from the Cradle of Jazz: New Orleans Music Since World War II* by Jason Berry, Jonathan Foose, and Tad Jones (2009), "Several important early musicians whom jazz writers have casually labeled 'Creole' were in fact of Mexican origin. At least two dozen." Musicians from Latin America and New Orleans continue to marry music and food.

Alexey's dish has Spanish origins but is a staple in Cuban cuisine. This dish adds crawfish, and it is truly amazing.

RUBENS LEITE

Rubens Leite (January 11, 1964, São Paulo, Brazil) migrated to New York City in the 1990s. In New York, he had a flourishing mobile food truck business that served street food to New York's five boroughs. Then Katrina struck in 2005 and a friend from New Orleans called Leite for help. Many of the construction workers who helped rebuild post-Katrina New Orleans were Latino. Leite recognized the need to feed the Hispanic workers food that was familiar to their palates. His menu changed from New York street food to Mexican food with a Brazilian touch. This type of street food was unfamiliar to New Orleans, and Leite was one of the first to introduce street tacos to the area. Throughout New Orleans, Leite's hand-painted colorful taco trucks fed a diverse clientele: tourists, late-night club hoppers, Latino construction workers, and service industry workers. His food can be tasted every night at Café Negril on Frenchmen Street. His success has also made him a celebrity. His trucks made a cameo appearance in HBO's *Tremé*.

I was born in São Paulo, Brazil, and I came to New York in 1991. I was an electronic engineer in Brazil and an electrician in New York. I didn't like it too much. One day I saw a food truck bring food to the construction workers. I liked how they got to meet new people every day. I bought my first truck and then a second truck and I started a small company. In New York I sold breakfast sandwiches and wedge sandwiches. Now I work with Mexican food in New Orleans. I changed a lot. When I came to New Orleans right after Katrina I brought my truck to feed the workers. I found that around 80 percent of the workers were Hispanic and they wanted their own food. I hired cooks and we made Mexican and Central American food. I enjoy it. Six years I have been here now. One day I was invited to a party and after the party I went to Frenchmen Street to go drink a beer. I parked my truck and people came up to my truck asking for food. I was out there for three or four years. It was a lot of fun. Sometimes a deejay would come out and play and people would

surround my truck and dance and enjoy eating the food outside. Everybody loved my burritos because they were cheap and filled you up. When you ask a Latin guy what is your favorite dish? The answer is all the same, food. I don't have my truck on Frenchmen; they gave me a lot of tickets even though I had all of the licenses. They arrested me every night and I got tired so I don't work the street anymore. Later, a friend invited me to use his kitchen at Café Negril and I set up there. A few years ago, I opened a restaurant in Gretna called Benny's Taqueria and another restaurant called The Palms near Tulane University. The students enjoy my restaurant. They go almost every night. A lot of friends I make. I make Mexican food, but I use my Brazilian way of doing food because we don't like too much spice. I don't like spicy food. I put some love in the food. I didn't open a Brazilian restaurant because we don't have enough Brazilians in New Orleans and it's expensive. We don't have menus in Brazil; they give you a card, green one side and red on the other then they bring the food to you. It can cost around fifty dollars and I don't think people in New Orleans want to pay that. I like New Orleans but I miss my country sometimes. You have maybe five hundred or eight hundred Brazilians in New Orleans. They are like gypsies. If they don't make money here they move to another city. When I was on Frenchmen Street, I served in my taco truck quesadillas, burrito, tacos. Pineapple pork taco was my best seller and pupusas and Honduran tamales. I have a regular menu, but we use the Brazilian flavor, less spice as possible so you can feel the flavor of the food. After they drink a lot, they eat the food and it's fresh so they feel the flavor of the food. Then they go home and go to sleep.

(Interview was translated from Spanish.)

Taco de Lechón de Piña
Pineapple Pork Taco

Makes about 2–3 servings: 1 hour prep time,
15 minutes cooking time

Ingredients

3-pound boneless pork loin, cut into ½-inch slices

1 teaspoon of Adobo seasoning

1 teaspoon of Cajun seasoning

1 jalapeño pepper, seeded and diced

2 garlic cloves, minced

1 cup of fresh pineapple, cut into small chunks

2 cups of pineapple juice

½ cup of red onion, finely diced

1 bunch of cilantro, finely chopped

6 corn tortillas

1 lime wedge

Preparation

Season sliced pork loin with Adobo and Cajun seasonings. In a bowl, marinate pork with pineapple juice, red onions, and garlic. Marinate for at least 1 hour but preferably overnight. Preheat outdoor grill on medium. Remove excess marinade and sauté pork slices for 4 to 6 minutes until caramelized. Do not overcook. In a bowl mix pineapple chunks, seeded and diced jalapeño, chopped cilantro, and diced red onions to make a salsa. Squeeze two limes over salsa and add a pinch of kosher salt. On a grill or electric/gas burner char tortillas on both sides rapidly. Use two taco shells per taco so they won't break. With a spoon, place pork mixture into each taco. Garnish with pineapple salsa, serve with a lime wedge.

Although New Orleans is known for being a restaurant culture, street food can be found at second line parades, tailgating parties, food festivals, and late at night on Frenchmen Street and St. Claude Avenue. (Frenchmen Street is where most locals hang out. It has a bohemian feel similar to the Wicker Park neighborhood in Chicago and Haight Street in San Francisco.) Historically, New Orleans's popular street food during the nineteenth and twentieth centuries consisted of pralines, tamales, hot sausage sandwiches, and hot dogs. After Hurricane Katrina, Latino food trucks and taqueria stands sprang up around the city. Many of the food truck owners opened up their own restaurants after some were continuously fined, which many of them considered harassment.

ANNA FRACHOU

Anna Frachou (December 14, 1982, Los Angeles, California) is the former director of marketing at Amerigroup Louisiana. Prior to joining Amerigroup, she served as the executive director of Puentes New Orleans, Inc., an organization focused on building assets and creating access for the Latino community in the greater New Orleans region. Within her three years at Puentes, Frachou founded the Puentes' Youth Leadership Initiative in the summer of 2009, organized a statewide U.S. census campaign in 2010, and spent her last year developing a regional Gulf Coast Leadership Academy for Latinos in the nonprofit sector in Alabama, Mississippi, and Louisiana. She served on the mayor-elect's Task Force on Youth and Families and the Recovery School District Community Task Force. She currently sits on the board of directors of Second Harvest Food Bank and was recognized and awarded the 2011 NFL Hispanic Heritage Leadership Award. Frachou earned her undergraduate degree from Loyola Marymount University in Los Angeles and completed her master's at Tulane University's Roger Thayer Stone Center for Latin American Studies in New Orleans.

Puentes means bridges and not only do we build bridges between the different ethnic communities in New Orleans; we also are building bridges from the past to the present. The history of New Orleans is very similar to the history of the Americas. The connection and relationship between the two needs to be embraced, remembered, and shared, as in one way or another, it becomes Our Story. My own history blends well into the social fabric that makes New Orleans and with that at Puentes, we continue to work toward strengthening the ties in this city, both socially and economically.

When I moved here in August of 2007 as a Latin American graduate student at Tulane University from Los Angeles, California, my mother came down with me. My mother at first glance of New Orleans said with her Cuban accent, "Oh my God! We're in Cuba!" When we first exited off of the highway after driving two days from California, she was in awe of how much it resembled her own

Cuba's famous dish ropa vieja, which literally translates in English to mean old clothes, was originally introduced to Cuba by Spanish sailors supposedly from the Canary Islands. Canary Islanders who immigrated to Cuba were known for their cattle training in Louisiana, and wealthy families in Cuba during the colonial era enjoyed variations of beef dishes. However, the preparation of ropa vieja was made by African slaves in Cuba, and bears a striking resemblance to West African cooking methods. Their use of tomatoes, peppers, and a seasoned achiote oil is different from the original Spanish version that used chickpeas and potatoes. In Anna's recipe she added her love for okra, which in Cuba is called *quimbombó*, an African term for okra. According to the book *A Movable Feast: Ten Millenia of Food Globalization* by Kenneth Kiple (2007), okra was brought from Africa to the Americas in the seventeenth century via the slave trade; but okra was used as far back as the twelfth century in Egypt. Okra is typically used in dishes in New Orleans, the Caribbean, and South America where African slaves were placed in captivity.

country. When we went out to eat for the first time after I unpacked, my mom ordered three New Orleans–style dishes. Just to taste the variety. I remember that we both loved shrimp Creole. It is definitely still one of my favorites. It is so similar to Cuban food which uses a sofrito, a sauce based in many Creole dishes and Cuban dishes and one that my mom makes frequently. However, what I love about this city is that I get to eat okra all the time and in abundance! I was first introduced to okra when I was a child, and I used to eat Campbell's gumbo soup out of the can. I was obsessed! I would eat it all the time. Sad but true. However, okra is eaten in Cuba; but I guess New Orleans was calling me from a young age.
(Interview was in the summer of 2009 while Anna Frachou was still director of Puentes.)

Ropa Vieja con Quimbombó
Old Clothes (Shredded Beef) with Okra

Makes about 5 servings: 30 minutes prep time, 45 minutes cooking time

Ingredients
1 pound of chuck roast
1 teaspoon of ground cumin
1 teaspoon of dried oregano
1 teaspoon of ground black pepper
1 teaspoon of sea salt

1 bay leaf

3 cups of chicken stock

1 can of tomato sauce

2 garlic cloves, finely diced

1 roasted green bell pepper

1 bag of frozen okra

Preparation

Puncture roast many times with a fork. Season roast with cumin, salt, and pepper. Pour 3 cups of chicken stock into a large stock pot, large enough to hold the roast. Add 1 bay leaf. When stock comes to a boil, add roast. Cook for 2 hours. If you need to add more water, add more until the roast is submerged almost completely. Boil roast until the meat is fork tender. Remove and let the roast rest for 15 minutes. Reserve liquid from the roast. With a fork tear meat up until the roast is completely shredded. Discard any fatty pieces. Do not discard liquid.

Roast 1 green bell pepper over the top grill or in the oven until blackened. Remove blackened skin. Remove seeds and slice into strips. Sauté 2 minced garlic cloves in olive oil at medium heat. Add 1 cup of the liquid from the boiled roast. Add 1 cup of tomato sauce, 2 bay leaves, 1 teaspoon of oregano, ground black pepper, ½ of the frozen okra from the bag. Taste the sauce. Reseason if need be. Pour sauce over shredded meat. Garnish with chopped parsley or cilantro. Serve with white rice and corn bread.

MARVA GARVIN

Marva Garvin (Bay Islands, Honduras) came to New Orleans as a young woman with her husband, Millet, when he was offered a job working for Tidewater Oil. They lived in the Ninth Ward on Gallier Street with Garvin's aunt when they first arrived. Garvin was a housewife for many years until she became a community activist for the largest Hispanic population in New Orleans, Hondurans. She is a member of the Honduras Association of Louisiana and the Bay Islands Committee. She has cooked for and organized several benefits, dinners, and dances, with money being donated to Honduras for medical clinics, hospital beds, sheets, and stethoscopes. She was awarded "Mother of the Islands" many times by the Bay Islands Committee. The food that she cooks always represents Honduras.

I was born in Bay Islands of Honduras. Guanaja Island to be specific. It was a small island of about ten-to-twelve thousand people. When I came to New Orleans with my husband we already knew how to speak English because it was taught in the schools on the islands. My husband, Millet, came to work as a seaman for Tidewater Oil in New Orleans to make a better living. There were a lot of Hondurans and other Latinos working as seamen at that time and still today. When we first moved to New Orleans we lived in the Ninth Ward on Gallier Street with my aunt. Back then it was a clean and nice neighborhood. We always cooked at every event we had for our community and the seamen. We eventually organized to help Hondurans here in New Orleans and back home. I am very proud of the charity work that we do here and the money we are able to raise from our benefit dinners and dances that allows us to send basic necessities back to Bay Islands for free because we purchased the boats here in the U.S. to ship it back home.

Casamiento a la Hondureña
Honduran Red Beans and Rice

Makes about 2 to 3 servings: 10 minutes prep time,
30 minutes cooking time

Ingredients

1 cup of dry red beans (submerge in a bowl of water
   overnight)

1 bay leaf

1 large onion, finely diced

⅓ cup of green bell pepper, chopped

1 mutton pepper (Honduran Bay Islands pepper),
   seeded and diced

2 cans of coconut milk

2 cups of water

2 cups of Zatarain's or parboiled long-grain rice

1 teaspoon of salt and freshly ground pepper

Preparation

In a medium-size pot, boil water. Add red beans and a bay
leaf. Boil for 2 hours or until red beans are semisoft. Drain red
beans into a colander. In the same pot add 2 tablespoons
of olive oil, peppers, and onion. Add salt and pepper. Sauté
until onion is translucent. Add rice. Toast for 2 minutes. Add
beans, milk, and water. Bring to a boil. Cover and cook rice at
a medium-low heat. Serve with *tostones* (fried plantains) and
fried fish.

Over one hundred thousand Hondurans lived in New Orleans right before Hurricane Katrina, making up about 10 percent of the population. Unlike many other Latino ethnic groups in other cities, Hondurans in New Orleans went almost unnoticed by the rest of the United States until Hurricane Katrina, when northern journalists reported on the largest Hispanic community in New Orleans. However, a 1962 article written by Bill Stuckey in the New Orleans *States-Item*, entitled "Largest United States Colony of Hondurans Here," gave New Orleans the name *Nacatamal*, a Honduran and Nicaraguan dish similar to the Mexican tamale that uses corn masa, meat, vegetables, and banana leafs for wrappers instead of corn husks.

The majority of Hondurans arrived in New Orleans during the middle part of the twentieth century because of their connection with United Standard Fruit Company and the political coups in the 1960s, and also during Hurricane Mitch in 1998 when ten thousand Hondurans were killed. Most Hondurans during the 1950s lived in what they called El Barrio Lempira, located in the Lower Garden District in Uptown New Orleans. El Restaurante Lempira was located on Magazine Street and was a favorite of the community during the 1960s and 1970s. On Napoleon Street there was another Honduran restaurant called Tipico that was known for its *sopa de mondongo* (tripe soup). El Barrio Lempira also had a bustling nightlife for the Honduran and Latino community where Honduran food like *sopa de caracol, pupusas, curtido, yucca con chicharrón,* and *tostones* were served daily. A large community of Garifunas from Honduras (West African descendants who were marginalized by mainstream Hondurans and lived in isolated communities where they were able to preserve their culture, language, and foodways) also came in the 1960s looking for better opportunities in the banana trade business when President Kennedy initiated the Alliance for Progress to develop economic relations between the U.S. and Latin America. The Garifunas settled in New Orleans East, Central City, and Uptown. Their culture and food is celebrated annually at the Misa Garifuna at St. Theresa's Catholic Church in New Orleans. Today, like most other Latino ethnic groups, the majority of Hondurans reside in Jefferson Parish, and many of their restaurants are now in Jefferson Parish and the West Bank; yet many of the Honduran elders have fond memories of El Barrio Lempira and the food that was made after mass, during festivals, dances, and in Honduran restaurants.

MARGARITA BERGEN WITH RAFAEL DELGADILLO

Margarita Bergen (April 24, 1946, Santo Domingo, Dominican Republic) came to New Orleans via New York in the 1980s. Bergen is a local celebrity and socialite. She is known for her flamboyant hats, her larger-than-life personality, and her love for New Orleans society. In January of 2012, she invited to her house her closest friends, myself, and Rafael Delgadillo, a local community organizer who made national headlines in September of 2010 after an attempted carjacking almost blinded him and left him with a bullet in his head. Bergen, with her love for life, and Delgadillo, with a renewed sense of purpose, ate their national Dominican dish, sancocho, and reflected on their lives and experiences in New Orleans.

I live to eat! For someone like me who lives to eat I learned early that I only have one stomach, so therefore I always cultivated the friendship of the best chef, the best sommelier, and the best waiter so when I go to a restaurant it will be the best

experience. They all know me. I will always have a glass of champagne, wine, or margarita in my hand. I'm from Santo Domingo but I was raised in La Romana. I come from a system in which you always had maids. I never made sancocho. I would go to the best chef in Santo Domingo who made sancocho. When I came from el colegio (boarding school) my grandmother said, "It is time for you to learn how to cook!" She said, "We first start the beans because it takes a long time." We started at 10 a.m.; it took us two hours. I left the kitchen after I put the beans and my grandmother said, "Where are you going, young lady?" I told her that I wanted to read something. She said, "You don't leave the kitchen until everything is finished. Oh, my God!" she said. "I don't want you to be like this other lady's daughter who got married and her maid ran away and she had to cook for her husband." My grandmother told me how the lady wanted to cook a chicken and she forgot to pull out las tripas. The chicken was beautiful until her

husband cut it and all of the guts came out and that is when the husband said you better go and pack your clothes because I am taking you home so that you learn how to cook! I love to cook nowadays. I love to have people to cook to.

Margarita talked about her growing up in New York, how she came to New Orleans and her passion for food and life.

I was sixteen when I left Dominican Republic. I grew up in New York. You would find me at Studio 54 when I lived there or at parties for the mayor. I was invited to every party. I had a beautiful body, 38, 24, 36. Everyone would remember what I wore. I went to college there and I have a B.S. in health education from Hunter College and two master's degrees in bilingual education from City College. I was one of the pioneers in bilingual education. I had broken up with my boyfriend while I lived in New York. I had a beautiful apartment near Central Park on 75th Street. He lived across the street from me and I knew I had to move. I had a broken heart. My brother, the artist, said, "Margarita, come to New Orleans!" So we both opened a gallery, Bergen Gallery on Royal Street. It's closed now. I lived in the heart of the French Quarter for twenty-three years on Royal Street. When I first came to New Orleans I thought it was going to be boring because I come from New York. But I found out there is so much going on in this

city. I am now a realtor and society editor for New Orleans Living Magazine. *I'm always busy. I was very fortunate because my boyfriend in New York was the editor of* Signature Magazine, *which was the magazine for the Diners Club. So my boyfriend kind of helped me cultivate the love for food. We researched the restaurant to make sure that it was the best and the dishes that we would try are the ones that were proven to be the best. I only like very good food. I cultivate the friendship of the chef. I like gumbo. I like the andouille seafood gumbo. But my favorite dish in New Orleans is the wonderful, wonderful barbecue shrimp at Mr. B's Bistro on Royal Street. They make the best! I also love the bread pudding soufflé at Commander's Palace. However, when I crave Dominican food I cook at home. I like to cook arroz con pollo, carne guisada, platanos. New Orleans is my home. I am so much a part of it. Very few things go on that I am not part of or invited to. I move well into the Latino community, the Americans, African Americans. I am a people person. It is not unusual for me to go to two and three parties in one night. Every day I get invitations from the gay and straight communities; that is why I could never leave New Orleans. I tried when I sold my gallery. I moved to Ibiza, Spain, and I realized that my body was in Spain but my mind was in New Orleans. Sometimes I would fly and pay nineteen hundred dollars just to come to New Orleans for a party. I had my license as a bartender so you*

see everything in my house is dedicated to cham-
pagne. My weakness! I have a long relationship
with champagne since I lived in New York. I was
the queen once of the Krewe of Cork for Mardi
Gras. Everyone knows my love for champagne. My
friend once gave me a big bottle of champagne that
cost $750. Life is too short, you have to enjoy! I love
the music! The food! The hospitality! The parties!
I wear a lot of hats and I am always on the go so I
need to be ready in a few minutes. Nothing covers
a bad hair day better than a hat. The thing that we
have here are pockets of Latinos so it isn't like New
York where you will find Dominicans in Corona
or Upper West Side. The majority of the people
here are Honduran. There are a lot of Latino
chefs working in the restaurants in New Orleans
and many are opening up their own restaurants.
Now that I am getting older I'm finding that my
stamina is changing. Until age fifty I would work
all day, take a nap, and go to the parties. The most
parties I ever did was seventeen parties in one day!
I had a chauffeured limousine. We would go and
they would say, "Why are we leaving?" and I would
say, "Darlings, we have another one to go to!"
When I go to parties I drink something, see people,
talk to people, and take photos. I know everybody.

Rafael Delgadillo (May 21, 1982, New York, New
York) and I first met in the summer of 2009.
We were both volunteering for LatiNola, a nonprofit organization that is a huge resource for
the Latino community in New Orleans. Rafael
and I always shared a love for the history of New
Orleans and its Latino presence. Whenever we
would see each other, I always walked away with
a greater understanding of the city and its history. I remember the day I found out that Rafael
had been shot in the fall of 2011. Like many of us
who have worked with him or are friends with
him, I was shocked and devastated, especially
since we had seen each other at an event the
prior week. Although violence in New Orleans
can sometimes be exaggerated when seen by people who live outside of the city, youth violence in
disadvantaged communities is a strong reality. So
when Rafael came for lunch at Margarita's house,
all we wanted to do was feed him sancocho to
help him heal quickly and hear his story. At one
point Margarita did spoon-feed him sancocho. It
was a memorable afternoon.

Like most Dominicans I was born in New York.
When I was six months old, we moved to Domini-
can Republic and the economy was plummeting in
the late eighties in the D.R., which is what we call
the Dominican Republic. When I was six years old,
we moved to New Orleans and my dad had some
friends that told him about some work they had
in New Orleans as salesmen. It was the summer
of 1988 and I have been here ever since. He made
the move and a few months later we moved, my
mother, myself, and my two sisters. My folks live

in Florida now. They were here for fourteen years. They moved ten years ago. I had just started college and my credits wouldn't have transferred to a school out there. I was twenty years old and I figured I was a big boy. I could do it on my own, but like so many Latinos they did end up leaving New Orleans, but they still love this place. They left for better jobs and better opportunities. It was a good decision for our family even though it split us up geographically. I majored in history at the University of New Orleans, and I also went there for graduate school. My focus was the Hispanic press in New Orleans in the nineteenth century. I got to be a part of an event in 2008 that celebrated the two hundredth anniversary of the first Hispanic newspaper to be published in the United States called El Misisipi *in 1808, right here in New Orleans. Since then there has been at least one Hispanic newspaper in New Orleans every decade to this day. That means there has been a continuous presence of Hispanics for two hundred years in the city of New Orleans. Historically, New Orleans was a Spanish colony. There were Spaniards here from the middle of the eighteenth century until 1803 when the Louisiana Purchase was passed. New Orleans was a Latin American city. In many ways it still is. It was on the perimeter of what we call Latin America. Until the Louisiana Purchase there was no Deep South. The Louisiana Purchase created the Deep South. New Orleans had its commercial relationships with Latin American*

cities—Havana, Santo Domingo, Campeche, Tampico, Veracruz, Caracas. If you think of the Gulf of Mexico and the Caribbean not just as bodies of water but as geographic places, then it forces you to understand that New Orleans has been a Latin American city even after the Louisiana Purchase. Today, we are a small population. No more than 10 percent of the current census. There was a surge of Hispanics migrating here after Katrina but we were here before Hurricane Katrina. Our history of the Hispanic press in New Orleans proves that. We used to say before the storm that our community was invisible. I wouldn't say that now, but we don't have any political capital. We were never part of the civic day-to-day of the city. Now we are more civically involved not because there is more attention on us. As far as the food connection goes with Latin America and New Orleans, if you are from the Caribbean like I am you see the food here and you know it has the same heritage—a mixture of African, European, and indigenous recipes and ingredients. One thing I like to tell people in New Orleans when they make a big deal about having red beans and rice on Mondays, I break their hearts when I tell them that in the Dominican Republic we eat red beans and rice every day. So much so we call it the Dominican Flag, La Bandera Dominicana. But don't get me wrong. I love the food here! I love po'boys and jambalaya. I'm not much of a seafood person. When I leave New Orleans I crave Patton's Hot Sausage. New

Orleans will always be home. I've realized that you don't necessarily have to live here for that to be the truth, but I'm alive now and I'm enjoying that.

Rafael spoke candidly about the day he was shot and his new outlook on life:

September 25, 2011, I was a victim of an attempted carjacking. I tried to speed off. They shot me. The bullet entered the back of my head; it is still lodged in my brain and will be there for life. I've survived. I'm living very well. I went blind for three days. I regained my vision about 90 percent of it. A lot of people called it miraculous. I was fortunate to see my own funeral while being alive. So many came out to raise money for my medical bills for a fund-raiser they had for me and a vigil to stop the violence in New Orleans. It made me realize that I must have been doing something right. So why should I leave? You don't get to pick when you come and go, you just live your life. I will continue to be a community organizer at Puentes New Orleans and help develop programs with the Latino population in the area. New Orleans is my home.

Sancocho a lo Dominicano
Dominican Sancocho

Makes about 8 to 10 servings: 40 minutes prep time, 2 hours cooking time

Ingredients

1 pound of beef shank, preferably with bones, cut into 1½-inch pieces

1½ pounds of skinned chicken thighs

1 pound of boneless pork shoulder, cut into 1½-inch pieces

2 large *naranja agria* or Goya Sour Orange Marinade (substitute with lemon)

1 pound of cassava or yucca, peeled and cut into large chunks

1 pound of white yam, peeled and cut into large chunks

1 pound of large potatoes, peeled and cut into large chunks

1 pound of eddoes or yautia, peeled and cut into large chunks

1 pound of chayote or mirliton, skinned and core removed, cut into large chunks

2 green plantains, peeled and cut into 1-inch rounds

1 Spanish pumpkin (calabaza) or butternut squash, seeded and skin removed, cut into large chunks

2 medium sweet corn ears, cut into 1½-inch rounds

5 liters of water

5 garlic cloves, finely minced

1 teaspoon of dried oregano

1 small bunch of cilantro, chopped

1 tablespoon of vinegar (optional)

Vegetable oil

1 green bell pepper, seeded and diced

1 cubanelle pepper, seeded and diced

3 large onions, finely diced

1 Caldo Maggi Carne or beef bouillon cube

1 Caldo Maggi Gallina or chicken bouillon cube

Salt and ground black pepper

3 cups of cooked white rice

1 ripe avocado, peeled and cut into slices

5 lime wedges

1 cup of cilantro, chopped

Serve with cooked white rice, avocado slices, lime, and chopped cilantro.

Note: All ingredients can be purchased at your local Hispanic or Caribbean grocery store. Make sure you ask the butcher to cut your meat if it is not already cut into large chunks.

Preparation

Remove the skin from the chicken and any excess fat from the other meats. Once you have done this, place all the meat in a large bowl and "wash" the meat again with *naranja agria* or lemon juice. Drain about half the liquid off. Season meat with 1 teaspoon of salt and ground black pepper. Set aside. Peel and cut the yucca, yam, potatoes, eddoes, chayote, plantains, and Spanish pumpkin about the same size as the meat. Cut the corn. Set aside. Mash garlic, cilantro, and oregano in a mortar and pestle. Put mixture into a bowl. Add a teaspoon of vinegar, vegetable oil, peppers, and chopped onions. Set aside. In an extra-large stock pot, add ½ cup of vegetable oil and brown all of the meat. Stir well. Add onion mixture. Stir well. Add five liters of water or until the water is past the halfway mark. Add bouillon cubes. Bring to a boil. Add yucca, yams, potatoes, and eddoes. Lower to a medium-high heat. Cook for 30 minutes. Add Spanish pumpkin, chayote, and corn. Cook for 1½ hours at a medium-low heat, stirring frequently. Add water if need be and salt and ground black pepper to taste. Serve with cooked white rice, avocado slices, and lime wedges. Garnish with chopped cilantro.

Sancocho is the beloved national dish of the Dominican Republic's gastronomy. It is our gumbo. It is one of those dishes that takes time and patience to make. We cook it on special occasions to share it with family or friends or when it is raining or cold outside. The original recipe calls for seven different kinds of meats but I think that it is practical to use beef, chicken, and pork—preferably with bones to flavor the soup. When I wanted to do this dish, I visited Ideal Supermarket on Broad Street in New Orleans where I found a great butcher shop and a great selection of Caribbean vegetables as well as the large avocados that I just love. Serve it with a nice cold Presidente (Dominican beer) and Tabasco sauce. Enjoy, darlings!
—Margarita Bergen

Sancocho originated in the Canary Islands and was brought by islanders when they immigrated to Latin America and South America.

LAGNIAPPE

Additional Recipes by Zella Palmer Cuadra

Lagniappe c'est bitin qui bon, a French term used in New Orleans during the nineteenth century, literally means lawful booty or something extra "given to purchasers of groceries, provisions of fruit or other goods sold at retail stores," according to Lafcadio Hearn's accounts of New Orleans culture in the late nineteenth century. However, the term originated from the Spanish word *la ñapa*, which was taken from the term *yapay,* the Quechua word for something extra during the conquest of the Incans. In both Louisiana and the Andean region, the practice of giving customers something extra is still commonplace.

This section includes my own recipes. The majority of the recipes in this section are a reflection of my upbringing in Chicago, my travels to various countries in Latin America, and my life in New Orleans. Like Lafcadio Hearn, I love food and I love to hear people's stories behind the food. I hope you enjoy my interpretation of my favorite cuisines, New Orleans and Latin American.

ENTRÉES

Paella de Camarones con Chorizo de Camaron
Seafood Paella with Shrimp Boudin

Makes about 3 to 4 servings: 20 minutes prep time, 40 minutes cooking time

Ingredients

½ cup of onion, diced

1 garlic clove, finely diced

⅓ cup of green bell pepper, diced

2 shrimp boudin links

1½ packets of Goya Sazon with Achiote (purchase at Latino grocery stores or in a major grocery store in the Hispanic section) or 1 tablespoon of tomato paste

1 teaspoon of ground cumin

2 cups of medium-grain white rice

3 cups of shrimp stock or chicken stock

1 pound of jumbo shrimp with heads on and tails removed (preferably Gulf shrimp)

½ pound of clams

1 red bell pepper, roasted and sliced

(Optional) Garnish with roasted red bell peppers, olives, and fresh chopped parsley or cilantro.

Preparation

Sauté garlic, green bell pepper, shrimp boudin, and onions in a paelleria or large pan. Add Sazon packets. Add rice and stir until all the rice is colored red and toasted for 2 minutes. Add shrimp stock. When the rice is almost done and the stock has almost evaporated, add the shrimp, clams, and capers. DO NOT STIR! Cover and cook on low-medium heat until rice is thoroughly cooked and the shrimp is pink and all clams have opened. Discard any clams that have not opened.

The Picayune's Creole Cook Book, originally published in 1901, referred to jambalaya, the famous New Orleans rice dish, as a Spanish-Creole dish. Over the years many have debated its origins and wondered if the Spanish paella was its direct descendant. Spain can lay claim to dishes from Catalonia, Spain, that use chickpeas and sausages. Many Catalan grocers lived in New Orleans during the Spanish rule of Louisiana. In this dish a simple paella recipe was used that acknowledges the Spanish love of sausages.

Camarones a la Criolla con Achiote
Achiote Shrimp Creole

Makes about 2 servings: 15–20 minutes prep time,
20 minutes cooking time

Ingredients

1 roasted green bell pepper, diced

1 pound of fresh medium-sized shrimp (preferably Gulf
   shrimp)

½ tsp of Adobo seasoning

½ of K-Paul's Seafood Magic

1 teaspoon of ground cumin

1 clove of garlic

¼ cup of Goya Achiote (annatto seeds) (purchase in Latino
   grocery stores)

⅓ cup of olive oil

1 celery stalk, diced

¼ cup of roasted green bell pepper

½ of a small yellow onion, diced

1 garlic clove, finely minced

2 tablespoons of shrimp stock or chicken stock

⅓ cup of cilantro

1 14.5-ounce can of Muir Glen Organic fire-roasted tomato
   sauce (substitute with 2 ripe Roma tomatoes; sear over
   cast-iron skillet until skin is blistered and then puree in a
   food processor, ¼ cup)

Preparation

Over medium heat on a stove gas burner or electric burner,
blister green bell pepper on all sides until black. (Monitor bell

pepper so that you don't cause a fire.) Set blistered bell pepper aside to cool. Remove shells and tails of the shrimp. Leave the heads on. Season shrimp with Adobo, Seafood Magic, and cumin. Take bell pepper and remove charred skin with the back of a knife and wipe bell pepper clean with a paper towel. Dice bell pepper. Heat 1 cup of olive oil in a small skillet and add ½ cup of achiote seeds. Toast for 1 minute until the oil starts to bubble. Drain oil into a colander. Pour oil into a ceramic bowl. Discard achiote seeds. Oil should be red. Be careful not to burn achiote seeds. Set aside. Sauté onions, garlic, celery, and bell pepper until translucent. Add stock, achiote oil, and 3 tablespoons of flour. Stir until the roux is a thick sauce consistency. Add tomato sauce. Cover and simmer for 20 minutes. Add shrimp and cook until shrimp is pink. Garnish with chopped cilantro. Serve over white rice.

According to the cookbook *A Taste of Cuba* by Linette Creen (1994), shrimp Creole, a classic dish in Cuba, was brought to Cuba following the Haitian revolution in 1791 when Haitian planters and their slaves fled Haiti. I would assume that the same dish was brought to New Orleans during the same time since so many Haitians migrated to Cuba and New Orleans. The dish uses fresh shrimp, a robust slow-cooked tomato sauce, and the nuttiness of achiote (annatto seed) to give it a Latin flavor.

Pernil de Cerdo Asado con Maiz Molido
Roasted Pork with Grits

Makes about 4 to 5 servings: 20 minutes prep time, 5 hours cooking time

Ingredients

3-pound pork leg or pork butt roast

3 squeezed sour oranges or 2 cups of Goya *naranja agria* (sour orange)

5 garlic cloves, finely diced

2 teaspoons of Goya Adobo seasoning

2 teaspoons of Creole seasoning

1 tablespoon of ground black pepper

1 tablespoon of ground cumin

1 box of quick grits

3 tablespoons of heavy cream

Preparation

Puncture pork with a sharp fork. Pour sour orange juice over pork. Put garlic in punctured holes with fingers. Season pork with Adobo, Creole seasoning, black pepper, and cumin. Cover and refrigerate overnight. Preheat oven to 400 degrees. Put a cooking thermometer in the pork. (The pork roast will be done when the thermometer is at 195 degrees Fahrenheit.) In a preheated oven, roast the pork in a deep pan for 4 to 5 hours. Lower temperature in the last 2 hours to 300 degrees F. Ladle orange marinade over the roast occasionally as it cooks. Broil for 2 minutes to get skin crispy. Let the pork rest for 30 minutes.

Follow grits directions on the box. Keep on medium-to-low heat and stir constantly. Do not leave grits unattended. Add 3 tablespoons of heavy cream. Salt and pepper to taste. Serve sliced pork over grits.

There is one thing that Louisiana and Latin Caribbean have in common: their love for pork. The Spanish, as early as the sixteenth century, brought pigs from Spain to their colonies and during their rule in Louisiana. Lechón asado, similar to the Cajun dish cochon de lait, is a slow-roasted marinated pork roast eaten throughout every former Spanish colony. This dish was served over grits, a southern staple.

Pollo Frito con Mojo
Southern Fried Chicken with Mojo Gravy

Makes about 2 to 3 servings: 10 minutes prep time,
15 minutes cooking time

Ingredients
1½ pounds of chicken thighs
4 cups of flour
2 cups of buttermilk
3 tablespoons of Spanish paprika
2 tablespoons of Adobo Goya Seasoning

⅓ cup of Cajun or Creole seasoning
⅓ cup of ground black pepper
½ cup of heavy cream
3 garlic cloves, minced
3 limes

Chicken preparation
Wash and rinse chicken. Let chicken marinate in a bowl of
buttermilk for an hour. Remove chicken from the bowl and
remove excess milk. Set aside. Mix flour and spices in a bowl.
Put flour mixture in a large paper bag and one chicken piece
at a time to coat with flour. In a deep fryer with peanut oil

or canola oil, fry chicken at 375 degrees until light golden brown. Do not overcrowd chicken in the oil. Set chicken on a paper towel.

Mojo gravy preparation

Mince 3 garlic cloves and sauté in a small pan. Add heavy cream and stir for 2 minutes. Season with salt and ground black pepper to taste. Remove and whisk in lime juice and stir. Drizzle over fried chicken and garnish chicken with finely diced cilantro or parsley.

> Fried chicken, a southern classic dish, was historically made by enslaved Africans in the southern region of the United States. Their use of seasonings and frying methods can be attributed to West Africa and their tradition of frying chicken in palm oil. Southern fried chicken is a favorite in New Orleans at restaurants like Dooky Chase and Willie Mae's Scotch House. Fried chicken is also very popular in Cuba in such restaurants as Comida Rapida. This dish uses the concept of smothered fried chicken but, adding a Cuban twist, a creamy mojo sauce substitutes for gravy.

Jibarito con Bistec a la Nueva Orleans
Chicago Puerto Rican Po'Boy with Grillades

Makes about 1 to 2 servings: 20 minutes prep time, 1 hour cooking time

Ingredients

1 large green plantain (hint: buy a few extra plantains just in case they break)
1 beef sirloin steak, thinly sliced
¼ cup of flour
¼ teaspoon of Adobo seasoning
¼ teaspoon of Creole seasoning
¼ teaspoon of salt and ground black pepper
⅓ cup of green bell pepper
⅓ cup of yellow onion, diced
⅓ cup of celery, diced
1 tablespoon of Worcestershire sauce
¼ teaspoon of dried thyme and oregano
1 ripe avocado, sliced
⅓ cup of lettuce, shredded
1 ripe tomato, thinly sliced
¼ cup of mayonnaise
2 garlic cloves, finely minced
2 limes, squeezed
⅓ cup of olive oil

Mojo sauce

5 garlic cloves, finely minced
⅓ cup of olive oil
3 limes, squeezed
Salt to taste

Preparation

Plantain

Cutting a plantain to make a jibarito can be difficult, but here is a trick. Take a sharp knife and cut down the seams of the plantain peel right up to the plantain meat. Take a knife or use your nail to peel the skin off. Once the peels are removed, slice the plantain horizontally in half. Put aside. Don't fry your plantain until you have cooked the meat and have all other ingredients ready to assemble the sandwich. Jibaritos taste best when the plantain is fresh out of the fry pan.

Meat

Tenderize the steak with a mallet. Season steak well with seasonings and then dredge the meat in flour. Over a medium flame fry steak with 3 tablespoons of canola oil. Flip the meat until golden brown. Remove the steak from the pan and set aside. Sauté the bell pepper, onion, and celery. Add 1 teaspoon of tomato paste. Add oregano, thyme, salt, and pepper. Add 1 tablespoon of Worcestershire sauce. Bring to a simmer. Add the steak. Cover and simmer on low heat for 30 minutes until fork tender.

While the steak is cooking, cut the lettuce, tomato, and avocado and have them ready to assemble the sandwich.

I grew up in Chicago, a city that is heavily influenced by Puerto Rican and Mexican culture. The jibarito, a fried plantain sandwich with meat, shredded lettuce, tomato, avocados, and mayonnaise and usually served with mojo sauce, was created in 1996 by Borinquen restaurant owner Juan "Pete" Figueroa. It is a Chicago favorite. I have fond memories of eating jibarito sandwiches with my friends and family at Borinquen and Papa's Cache Sabroso restaurant in Humboldt Park, a historic Puerto Rican neighborhood.

When I moved to New Orleans in 2009, I craved this dish more than anything else that I grew up eating in Chicago. Every time I went back to Chicago for the holidays I had to make a pit stop at Papa's Cache Sabroso for their jibarito with a side of arroz con gandules (Puerto Rican rice with pigeon peas) and extra mojo. I thought it would be interesting to combine my love for jibaritos and one of my favorite dishes for brunch in New Orleans, grillades (usually served over grits). Grillades, a Creole classic that was created after World War II in the African American community in New Orleans during hard times, is similar to bistec empanizado (breaded steak) but with a smothered gravy. Grillades was used in this dish as the meat component. As with the Germans who came to New Orleans and added potato salad to their gumbo, I am adding the concept of a jibarito sandwich to grillades. Every time I make this dish it takes me back to Humboldt Park in Chicago and eating jibaritos with the ones I love.

Make the mojo sauce. In a small bowl add ⅓ cup of olive oil, 2 finely minced garlic cloves, and juice of 2 squeezed limes. Whisk and set aside.

Fry the cut plantain in canola oil at 275 degrees. Remove the plantain when slightly golden brown. Place both sliced plantains on a wooden chopping board and take the back of a cast-iron skillet or mallet and smack the plantain until it looks like an oval pancake. Be careful not to use too much force or risk breaking the plantain. I always buy more than one plantain at the grocery store just in case it breaks. Re-fry until crispy golden brown. Place on a paper towel and pat dry.

Mojo sauce
Mix all ingredients together thoroughly. Serve as a side sauce with the jibarito.

Assemble sandwich
Spread a small amount of mayonnaise on the plantain as you would a sandwich. Add the grillade steak, shredded lettuce, tomato, and sliced avocado. Drizzle mojo sauce over the grillade. Cut sandwich in half on a slant carefully. Serve with a salad and/or arroz con gandules.

Chicharrónes con Yucca Frita
Grattons with Yucca Fries

Makes 3 servings: 30 minutes prep time,
5 to 10 minutes cooking time

Ingredients
1 pound of a cut of pork with meat, fat and skin attached
   (purchase in most Latin American grocery stores or a
   butcher shop)
½ cup of peanut oil or canola oil
1-pound bag of Goya frozen yucca
1 teaspoon of Cajun seasoning
Salt
3 limes

Preparation
Thaw frozen yucca. Cut into large fries and fry in canola or
peanut oil. Set aside. Cut pork meat into large cubes. Fry in
about ½ cup of peanut oil or canola oil in a large black cast-
iron pot. Remove cracklins' when lightly brown and the yucca
fries are golden brown. Place on paper towel. Season with
Cajun seasoning and a cut lime.

Grattons, similar to chicharrónes in Latin America,
is a Cajun dish of fried pork rinds. Families would
use every part of the pig for consumption. In New
Orleans at Donald Link's restaurant Cochon, grattons are served on the daily menu, and they are
sold at most Latino grocery stores. This is my family's recipe that is served with yucca fries but seasoned with Cajun seasoning similar to Cajun fries.

Chayote Rellenos
Stuffed Mirlitons

Makes about 6 servings: 40 minutes prep time,
1 hour cooking time

Ingredients

½ pound of ground beef

2 limes, squeezed

1 tablespoon of Adobo seasoning

¼ teaspoon of salt and ground black pepper

1 teaspoon of low-sodium Creole seasoning

4 mirlitons or chayote

1 large onion, finely chopped

3 cloves garlic, minced

2 tablespoons of tomato paste

½ pound of uncooked shrimp, chopped into chunks

3 tablespoons butter

1 cup seasoned Italian bread crumbs

1 teaspoon of fresh parsley, chopped

1 teaspoon of cilantro, chopped

¼ cup of bread crumbs

2 tablespoons of grated Parmesan cheese

6 teaspoons of butter

Preparation

Marinate ground beef with juice of 2 squeezed limes,
1 tablespoon of Adobo seasoning, and ¼ teaspoon of both
salt and pepper in a bowl. In another bowl mix chopped
shrimp with Creole seasoning. Boil whole mirlitons for
approximately 1 to 1½ hours until they are fork tender. Reserve

When I first moved to New Orleans in 2009, a Creole friend of mine invited me to her home for dinner. When she served her guests stuffed mirlitons it immediately took me back to eating chayote in México when I was a little girl during a long stay there with my family. Many of her guests never knew that mirlitons actually came from México and that they are used in many dishes in Latin America. According to Kenneth Kiple's book *A Movable Feast: Ten Millenia of Food Globalization* (2007), the chayote or mirliton "was domesticated in México and became established in Peru after the conquest." Mirliton dishes have been part of Creole/Cajun cuisine throughout Louisiana since the nineteenth century and chayote in México for centuries. This dish is what I would consider a Creole/Criolla dish as the late Creole chef Austin Leslie noted in the book *Austin Leslie's Creole-Soul* by Austin Leslie and Marie Rudd Posey (2000): "Here's what happens when Caribbean squash meets with pure Creole-Soul." I agree.

½ cup of mirliton liquid. Drain in a colander and cool for a few minutes. Remove seeds and pulp with a spoon and reserve in a bowl. Do not discard the mirliton shells. Preheat the oven to 375 degrees. Sauté ground beef in a skillet until browned on both sides but not completely cooked. Drain meat into a colander. In the same skillet sauté chopped onions and garlic in 2 tablespoons of oil. Add 2 tablespoons of tomato paste and about ¼ cup of the reserved mirliton liquid. Simmer on low heat until the sauce thickens. Add more mirliton liquid if necessary. Add meat mixture and ½ cup of the mirliton pulp. Cook for 10 minutes until the meat is cooked. In a separate pan sauté shrimp in butter until the shrimp turns pink. Do not overcook. Mix meat and mirliton mixture with shrimp. Add bread crumbs, parsley, cilantro, and Parmesan cheese. With a large spoon scoop the mixture into the mirliton shells. Sprinkle tops with bread crumbs and Parmesan cheese and small bits of butter, about 2 teaspoons for each mirliton. Put shells into a deep casserole dish. Bake for 25 minutes.

APPETIZERS

Ostiones con Pica de Gallo
Oysters with Pica de Gallo

Makes about 6 servings: 15 minutes prep time,
10 minutes cooking time

Ingredients
2 bags of fresh oysters (preferably Louisiana oysters),
    about 12 to 14 in total
1 Creole or 2 Roma tomatoes
¼ cup of fresh corn kernels
1 jalepeño pepper, seeded and minced
⅓ cup of red onion, finely diced
⅓ cup of cilantro, finely chopped
1 squeezed lime
Sea salt and freshly ground black pepper to taste

Preparation

Pica de gallo
Finely chop onions, cilantro, and tomato(es). Put into a
bowl. Add corn and jalepeño. Squeeze lime. Add a pinch
of sea salt and black pepper to taste and mix with a large
spoon. Set aside.

Oysters

Scrub the oyster shells with a bristle brush under tepid water. Discard any oysters that are already opened. Use a towel or oven mitt to hold oysters as you shuck them. Shuck oysters over a bowl. Insert slowly an oyster knife or butter knife at the seams of the oyster. Gently twist the knife back and forth to pry the shell open. Using the knife, cut the muscle away from the top shell, bend the shell back, and discard it. Place the shucked oysters on a bed of crushed ice or rock salt. Serve oysters on a platter with a teaspoon of the pica de gallo for a garnish.

Oysters are in abundance in Louisiana thanks to the Gulf of México that provides the region with fish and shellfish. There are so many different ways to prepare them: grilled, raw, fried, or broiled. In New Orleans, the famous Oysters Rockefeller and Oysters Bienville are still favorites at fine dining restaurants in the French Quarter. *The Picayune's Creole Cook Book* (1901) proudly gives New Orleans sole ownership for introducing the many ways to prepare oysters to the rest of the United States. However, in México, specifically coastal cities like Veracruz that once had strong ties with New Orleans, they too have oysters in their culinary traditions. This recipe uses pica de gallo, a fresh salsa, to top off raw oysters.

Mangu con Beicon y Salsa de Tomate a la Criolla
Mangu with Bacon and Creole Tomato Dressing

Makes about 2 servings: 10 to 15 minutes prep time, 30 to 45 minutes cooking time

Ingredients

1 Creole ripe tomato or 2 Roma tomatoes
1 clove of garlic
Creole mustard
1 tablespoon of mayonnaise
½ tablespoon of Creole mustard
1 teaspoon of Creole seasoning
4 green plantains
½ cup of milk
2 tablespoons of butter
4 slices of cooked bacon
Cilantro (optional)
Salt and pepper to taste

Preparation

Creole Tomato Dressing
In a food processor or blender, blend tomato, garlic, Creole mustard, mayonnaise, and Creole seasoning. Taste and adjust seasoning if necessary. Set aside.

Mangu

Boil a large pot of water. Remove plantain peels and chop plantains into large chunks. Season the water with 2 pinches of salt. Boil plantains until fork tender. Drain and reserve plantain liquid in a colander. Mash plantains with a potato masher. Add in 1 cup of the reserved plantain liquid a little bit of water at a time. Warm ½ cup of milk in the microwave for 1 minute and mix into plantain mash. Mix in butter. Add salt and pepper to taste and ladle Creole tomato dressing over the mangu. Garnish with cooked chopped bacon (cilantro optional).

I ate mangu for the first time at a friend's house when I visited the Dominican Republic in 2003. I fell in love with the richness of this mashed plantain dish. Preparation is similar to that of mashed potatoes. Mangu is a favorite in Dominican cuisine and is eaten in many Dominican households in New Orleans. This dish uses the concept of mangu but is topped with Creole tomato dressing and bacon.

Frijoles Rojos con Tortillas Frita
Red Bean Dip with Homemade Tortilla Chips

Ingredients

Leftover red beans or 1 small can of red beans (if you don't
  have leftover beans then you need to puree a can of red
  beans in a food processor)
1 package of corn tortillas
Canola oil
Salt and pepper to taste
Sauté trinity: ⅓ cup of diced celery, ⅓ cup of finely diced
  yellow onion, and ⅓ cup of diced green bell pepper. Add
  1 minced garlic clove. Season with 1 teaspoon of Creole
  seasoning. Add beans and adjust seasoning. Cool and
  refrigerate for 1 hour.

Preparation

Puree leftover red beans in a food processor. Put in a bowl and
refrigerate. Heat 2 cups of canola oil in a deep frying skillet
at medium heat. Cut corn tortillas like a pizza. Test the oil to
make sure it bubbles. Fry tortillas until golden brown. Remove
tortillas from the oil and place on an absorbent paper towel.
Serve red bean dip and tortillas on dip platter.

Monday was traditionally wash day for women in New Orleans during the nineteenth and part of the twentieth centuries. Women would slow-cook red beans over the stove while washing clothes by hand. Red beans were most likely brought after the Haitian revolution when many Haitians were exiled in New Orleans. Red beans are eaten throughout Latin America. This dish was made to extend red beans after Monday by the creation of a dip with fresh tortilla chips.

Croquetas de Camarones y Langostina con Salsa Verde
Shrimp and Crawfish Croquette with Creamy Salsa Verde

Makes up to 30 croquetas: 30 minutes prep time, 10 minutes cooking time

Ingredients

Croquetas:
3 pounds of ham, cooked and diced
1 yellow onion, diced
2 red bell peppers, diced
2 cloves of garlic, crushed
2 tablespoons of tomato paste
½ cup of parsley, chopped
½ cup of cilantro
½ teaspoon of nutmeg
1 teaspoon of cumin
1 teaspoon of Creole seasoning
¼ teaspoon salt and ground black pepper
½ cup of flour
½ cup of heavy cream
½ cup of thawed frozen crawfish tails or ½ cup of cooked small shrimp
1 cup of bread crumbs
¼ cup of Parmesan cheese
4 eggs

Preparation

Sauté with a little olive oil ham, onions, peppers, garlic, and tomato paste in a pan until onions and peppers are soft. Add chopped parsley, cilantro, spices, salt and pepper, and cream. Sprinkle in flour. Remove. In a food processer mix ham mixture until completely blended. Pour in heavy cream. Remove mixture from the food processor and fold the crawfish tails in with a spoon.

Take bread crumbs and Parmesan cheese and pour into a deep-dish bowl. Put aside. In another deep-dish pan whisk 4 cracked eggs in with a fork. Lightly move the croqueta in the egg bath. Dip the croqueta in the bread crumb mixture. Refrigerate for 4 hours or overnight or freeze for use a few days later. Fry until golden brown in a deep fryer or a deep cast-iron pot with canola or peanut oil.

Creamy salsa verde

Ingredients

¼ cup of cilantro

¼ cup of parsley

1 clove of garlic

⅓ cup of olive oil

1 squeezed lime

Salt and ground black pepper to taste

Preparation

In a food processor pulse a handful of cilantro and parsley. Add 1 garlic clove. Pulse. Add juice of 1 squeezed lime. Pulse. Add the olive oil a little bit at a time and lightly mix. Remove sauce from the food processor and add salt and ground black pepper to taste. Serve with the croquetas.

Croquetas originally came from France but became a classic Spanish tapas dish and a Cuban tradition for weddings and festivals. Traditionally, Cuban croquetas are made with ham and have much more flavor than some of the Spanish recipes. This dish is made with crawfish and is served with a creamy salsa verde.

Elote a la Parilla con Mantequilla de Langostina
Grilled Corn with Crawfish Butter

Makes about 2 to 3 servings: 10 minutes prep time, 10 minutes cooking time

Ingredients

4 ears of fresh sweet corn
¼ teaspoon of cayenne pepper
¼ teaspoon of chili powder
2 sticks of salted butter
½ cup of crawfish tails
1 teaspoon of Creole seasoning
1 tablespoon of cilantro, chopped

When I was in México as a little girl and even in Chicago, grilled corn prepared by Mexican street vendors was a popular street food and still is. Mexican-style street corn is usually topped with mayonnaise, cotija cheese, and chili powder. Cajun cuisine in Louisiana, which has influences from México and from Native Americans in Louisiana, uses corn in various ways such as corn maque choux and in crawfish boils with potatoes. This dish refers to my love for grilled corn in my childhood and uses crawfish butter as a substitute for mayonnaise.

Preparation

Remove husks from corn. Coat corn ears with olive oil lightly with a brush. On a grill or with a cast-iron pan on the stove, cook corn until kernels are lightly browned. In a food processor mix butter, crawfish tails, Creole seasoning, cayenne pepper, chili powder, and cilantro. Spread crawfish butter evenly over corn and serve with lime wedges.

Ensalada de Aguacate con Vinagre de Fresa
Avocado Watermelon Salad with Louisiana Strawberry Vinaigrette

Makes about 1 to 2 servings: 10 minutes prep time

Ingredients

3 ripe avocados

2 cups of seedless watermelon chunks

1 cup of strawberries (preferably Louisiana)

1 tablespoon of balsamic vinegar

Freshly ground black pepper and salt

Preparation

Cut watermelon into chunks and put into a large mixing bowl. Cut avocados in half and remove seeds. With a knife cut around the edges of the avocado meat. Cut horizontally three times down the avocado meat and then cut vertically into large chunks. With a large spoon remove the avocado meat. Do not discard the avocado shells. Set aside. Puree strawberries in a food processor. Add balsamic vinegar and salt and pepper to taste. Fold the avocados and watermelon with the strawberry vinaigrette. With a large spoon place avocado salad into the avocado shells and serve.

When in season, Louisiana strawberries are some of the sweetest that I have ever tried. They are much smaller and are not hollow like California strawberries. In this dish I used Louisiana strawberries to make a vinaigrette dressing, with watermelon, a southern favorite in summer months, and avocado, a Latin American staple. When I made this dish I bought the ingredients from some local Mexican farmers at the Gretna Farmer's Market. In small talk, I learned from them that in 2008, a group of Mexican strawberry pickers made national headlines when they organized and sought out help from some local organizations after being treated inhumanely. Many were brought to Louisiana as cheap labor to work at a strawberry farm outside of New Orleans. Many organized and served as an example for Latino guest workers who come to Louisiana during economic hardships in their own countries. Fortunately, a number of nonprofit organizations work tirelessly to make sure that Latino migrant farm workers in Louisiana get fair treatment. These organizations include the Alliance of Guest Workers for Dignity, Latino Farmers Cooperative of Louisiana, and the Black Alliance for Just Immigration.

Tomate Verde Frito con Ceviche Hondureño
Fried Green Tomatoes with Honduran Ceviche

Makes about 1 to 3 servings: 15 minutes prep time,
30 minutes cooking time

Ingredients

1 package of seafood mixta (purchase at Latino grocery store)
or ⅓ cup of fresh calamari, oysters, clams, and shrimp

1 serrano pepper, seeded and diced

1 red bell pepper, diced

⅓ cup of red onion, diced

⅓ cup of cilantro, finely chopped

1 orange

1 lime

¼ teaspoon of sea salt

¼ teaspoon of freshly ground pepper

1 tight large container or fastened jar

3 large green tomatoes

½ cup of buttermilk

½ cup of flour

½ cup of cornmeal

1 tablespoon of K-Paul's Vegetable Magic

2 cups of canola oil

Preparation

Dice red bell pepper, red onion, serrano pepper, and cilantro. Place in a bowl and mix with seafood mixture. Squeeze the lime and orange. Add salt and pepper. Spoon ceviche into a canning jar and fasten. Chill in the refrigerator for 1 hour.

Cut green tomatoes into thick slices. In a bowl add ½ cup of buttermilk. In another bowl mix cornmeal, flour, and 1 tablespoon of K-Paul's Vegetable Magic. In a large frying pan, heat canola oil to a medium-high heat. Test the oil with a teaspoon of cornmeal mixture to see if it rises to the top and bubbles. Dip tomato slices into buttermilk. Shake off lightly any excess milk. Lightly dip the green tomatoes into the cornmeal mixture. Make sure each tomato slice is covered with cornmeal mixture. Fry until golden brown and pat dry with a paper towel. Spoon ceviche over each fried green tomato slice.

Fried green tomatoes are a favorite in the South, yet the origins of this dish are still being debated. According to culinary historian Robert F. Moss, author of *Barbecue: The History of an American Institution* (2010), fried green tomatoes is actually a northern dish made by Jewish immigrants. The first mention of fried green tomatoes was in a Dayton, Ohio, Presbyterian cookbook in 1873. Nevertheless, many New Orleans restaurants and the annual Creole Tomato Festival feature fried green tomatoes on their menus, usually served with a scoop of shrimp remoulade. This recipe replaces shrimp remoulade with ceviche, a Central American and South American dish that uses raw fish and citrus fruits as a cooking agent. According to Peruvian chef Gastón Acurio, author of *500 años de fusión* (*500 Years of Fusion*, 2008), ceviche originated in Peru and was brought to the Americas by the Spanish colonizers. In the New Orleans area, pupuserias, which literally means where pupusas (tortillas stuffed with meat, cheese, and beans) are sold, are more traditionally found on the West Bank at places like the Pupuseria Buen Gusto restaurant on Lapalco Boulevard in Harvey, Louisiana.

SOUPS AND ONE-POT MEALS

Mofongo de Gumbo
Gumbo Mofongo

Makes up to 6 servings: 30 minutes prep time,
2 hours cooking time

Ingredients
4 green plantains
1 clove of garlic, finely minced
¼ cup of pork cracklins' (chicharrónes), made or
    bought (optional)

Gumbo
1 cup of peanut oil (vegetable oil if allergic)
2 tablespoons of salted butter
1 cup of flour
½ cup of celery, diced
½ cup of green pepper, diced
1 cup of yellow onion, diced
¼ cup of garlic, diced
½ cup of andouille sausage
3 quarts of seafood or chicken stock
3 bay leaves
1 cup of frozen sliced okra
2 large crabmeat claws
1 pound of medium-sized raw shrimp, peeled
1 cup of green onions, chopped
1 cup of fresh parsley, chopped

To make the gumbo

Chop all your ingredients and have them ready to be put in a large stock pot.

First you make a roux. Take 1 cup of peanut oil and 1 cup of flour and cook over medium-low heat in a large pot, constantly stirring. Never leave your roux! Stir until the roux turns the color of a dark penny. Add butter, celery, green pepper, and onion. Cook until translucent. Add garlic. Do not burn garlic. Season with Creole seasoning. Add andouille sausage and cook for a few minutes. Add 3 quarts of seafood stock. Bring to a boil. Add okra and stir. Bring to a simmer and add 3 bay leaves. Add more stock or water if the gumbo gets too thick. Cover and simmer at a low-medium heat for 1 hour. Turn off the heat and add 2 large crabmeat claws and 1 pound of medium raw shrimp. Cover. Garnish with chopped green onions and parsley.

Mofongo

While the gumbo is cooking, peel and cut plantains. Cut on a slant into large chunks about 1 inch thick. Fry in canola oil until slightly browned.

Remove and place on a paper towel. In another pan sauté garlic in olive oil for a few minutes. Remove. Mash fried plantains with pestle into a large mortar or wood bowl until fully covered like a bread bowl. Use olive oil to help you press the mofongo onto the sides of the mortar or bowl. Mash with fingers the garlic and cracklins' into the mofongo. Set aside. When the gumbo is ready, pour into the mofongo bowl. Serve immediately.

Mofongo is traditionally a Puerto Rican dish with African origins and is also one of my favorite dishes that I ate when I was younger growing up in Chicago and visiting family in New York during vacations. Mofongo is made from fried green plantains mashed together with pork cracklins', sofrito (similar to pesto sauce), broth, garlic, and achiote oil. It can be served with a seafood, chicken, beef, or vegetable stew to resemble a bread bowl soup. For this dish, I applied the concept of mofongo but used a revised version from my friend and chef-in-residence at the Southern Food & Beverage Museum, Stephanie Carter, with gumbo instead of a traditional Puerto Rican stew. Buen Provecho!

Sopa de Pollo a lo Cubano con Chayote
Cuban Chicken Soup with Mirliton

Ingredients

1 whole chicken, cut into pieces and skinned, or a store-
   bought rotisserie chicken, deboned, skin removed, and
   chopped into chunks
4 quarts of water
1 cup of large cut chunks of peeled malanga root
1 cup of large cut chunks of peeled potatoes
1 cup of large cut chunks of peeled eddoe or yautia

1 cup of large cut chunks of peeled mirliton (chayote)
1 cup of large cut chunks of Spanish pumpkin or
   calabaza
2 tablespoons of olive oil
5 garlic cloves, finely minced
2 tablespoons of tomato paste
1 tablespoon of cumin
1 teaspoon of salt and ground black pepper
1 teaspoon of Adobo seasoning
½ cup of Mexican fideos (thin vermicelli soup noodles)
3 lime wedges

Note: All major Hispanic or Caribbean grocery stores carry root vegetables, mirlitons (chayote), Spanish pumpkins, seasoning, and fideos. When peeling root vegetables use a potato peeler and a large sharp knife to cut them into chunks. They can be tough to cut.

Preparation

Chop and peel all root vegetables. Set aside in a large bowl. With a sharp knife remove the shell of the Spanish pumpkin, cutting as you would a watermelon. Discard seeds and cut into large chunks. Set aside in a bowl. In a large stock pot sauté minced garlic with olive oil on low heat for a couple of minutes. Do not burn! Add tomato paste and seasoning. Add chicken and sauté for a couple of minutes. Add more olive oil if need be. Add 4 quarts of water to the stock pot. Bring to a boil at a medium-high heat. Add eddoe (yautia), malanga, potatoes, and mirliton (chayote). Cook for about 30 minutes. When the root vegetables are almost fork tender add the Spanish pumpkin and the fideos. Cook for an additional 15 minutes. Serve in a soup bowl. (Optional) Garnish with chopped cilantro and serve with lime wedges.

There is nothing like chicken soup *a lo Cubano!* I have fond memories of visiting family in Cuba for the first time and eating a hot bowl of Cuban chicken soup. I dedicate this recipe to Yanetsy, my son's aunt who taught it to me. As with the Dominican sancocho, root vegetables are used to make this hearty chicken soup. In this dish, similar to gumbo that includes African and indigenous influences, the taro root vegetables and yams are of African origin and the calabaza or Spanish pumpkin are of Taíno Indian origin. The Spanish also have their influences in this dish; cumin, a heavily used spice in Cuban cuisine, garlic, and limes were all brought to the Americas by the Spanish. This dish typically does not use mirlitons or chayote but it still has indigenous influences of the Americas. Chicken Soup *a lo Cubano!* continues to be a favorite in every Cuban household.

DESSERTS

Pralines con Ron
Rum Pralines

Ingredients

2 cups of refined white sugar

1 cup of light brown packed sugar

1½ cups of chopped pecans

6 tablespoons of butter

½ cup of milk

½ teaspoon of pure vanilla extract

1 tablespoon of dark rum or rum extract

1 sheet of parchment paper

Preparation

In a steel or aluminum medium-size pot, add sugars, pecans, butter, milk, and rum. Once the praline mixture comes to a roaring boil turn a timer on for 3 minutes. Stir one or two times. Remove the pot from the heat and place the pot on a

The Persians in the seventh century refined sugarcane cultivation, and when they were conquered by the Arabs in the ninth century, they established sugarcane plantations. Seven centuries later, the Spanish and Portuguese took sugar cultivation to their colonies along with African slaves. In Cuba and in Louisiana sugar was king. In her book *Degrees of Freedom: Louisiana and Cuba after Slavery* (2005), Rebecca J. Scott stated, "In Central Cuba it spread up along the rivers, in South Louisiana it came down the bayous. Cane covered the land . . . men with capital laid their hands on men and women with neither capital nor legal freedom, and together they changed the landscape." Rum, an alcohol made as a sugarcane product, was created in the Caribbean by African slaves and, according to a 1770 Louisiana tax decree by Governor Alexander O'Reilly, was imported heavily from Cuba to the ports of New Orleans. The praline, a New Orleans caramel pecan candy, was inspired by an almond candy made by Marshal du Plessis-Praslin, a cook in France during the antebellum period. *Marchandes*, black female street vendors in New Orleans, sold pralines around Congo Square and near St. Louis Cathedral throughout the end of the nineteenth century and into part of the twentieth century. Pralines are still a favorite candy in New Orleans, and they are still sold throughout the French Quarter and during second lines. This recipe is a dedication to what Rebecca J. Scott in her book called *Two Worlds of Cane*.

marble surface or on a cool burner. Stir with a wooden spoon until the praline mixture turns into a milky creamy consistency. On parchment paper tilt the pot with the handle up for comfort and easy access to the pot. Using a wooden spoon, dollop the praline mixture as with small cookies. Let the pralines cool. Serve.

Pudín de Pan con Salsa de Tres Leche
Tres Leche Bread Pudding

Ingredients

1 10-ounce loaf of stale French bread, crumbled

2 cups of sugar

3 eggs

2 teaspoons of good vanilla

2 teaspoons of ground cinnamon

Tres Leche Glaze

1 14-ounce can of sweetened condensed milk

1 12-ounce can of evaporated milk

1 cup of half and half

Tres Leche Topping

2 cups of heavy cream

1 teaspoon of vanilla

1 tablespoon of sugar

(Optional) 1 ripe peeled mango pureed with 1 teaspoon of sugar

Preparation

Preheat the oven to 350 degrees. In a large bowl crumble bread into large chunks. In another bowl mix eggs, sweetened condensed milk, evaporated milk, half-and-half, sugar, vanilla, and cinnamon. Fold milk mixture into the bread. The bread pudding should be very moist but not soupy. Bake bread pudding in a 9 x 12 buttered baking dish for 1 hour. Whisk or blend with a hand mixer 2 cups of heavy cream, 1 teaspoon of vanilla, and 1 tablespoon of sugar until it becomes a meringue consistency. After the bread pudding has cooled for 15 minutes spread the topping over the bread pudding. (Optional) Cut the peels off of a ripe mango and puree in a blender with 1 teaspoon of sugar. Drizzle mango puree over the bread pudding.

Bread pudding has been a New Orleans favorite dessert since the late nineteenth century. Both *The Creole Cookery* (1885) and *La Cuisine Creole* by Lafcadio Hearn included bread pudding recipes. A dessert that is part of a culture that wastes nothing, it is still served in New Orleans to this day but usually comes with a whiskey butter sauce. My version uses a tres leche sauce and topping. Tres leche literally means three milks and is a sponge cake that probably originated in northern Spain where many dishes were created from dairy products. Some historians believe that tres leche cake was created in Nicaragua in the late nineteenth century. It is a popular dessert in Puerto Rico, Central America, and México.

Tostones Rellenos con Queso de Chivo y Beicon de Praline
Stuffed Plantains with Goat Cheese and Praline Bacon

Makes about 4 servings: 15 minutes prep time, 15 minutes cooking time

Ingredients
4 green plantains
2 ounces of goat cheese
2 strips of cooked bacon
⅓ cup of pecans, finely minced
2 tablespoons of brown sugar

Preparation
With a sharp knife cut the plantain down the seams of the peel. Gently place the knife under the peel to remove the peels. Cut the plantains on a slant about ½ inch apiece. Fry in canola oil at medium-high heat. When the plantain gets golden brown, remove it and begin to shape the plantain with your thumbs into a small bowl. Fry one more time for

three seconds until light golden brown. Place fried plantain shells on a dry paper towel. Then dice the two strips of bacon. In a food processor or coffee grinder chop ⅓ cup of pecans until they are very fine. Fry bacon in a pan with pecans and 2 tablespoons of brown sugar until bacon is thoroughly cooked. Remove praline bacon mixture from the pan and set aside in a bowl. Take about a tablespoon of goat cheese and place it in the middle of the plantain shell and top each shell with the praline bacon mixture.

This is a contemporary dish that I made up after eating with friends at Elizabeth's restaurant in the Bywater neighborhood in New Orleans where they serve a mouth-watering blue cheese burger with praline crusted bacon. Tostones rellenos are typically made in Cuba, Puerto Rico, and the Dominican Republic. They are usually stuffed with seafood, chicken, or beef, but in this dish I wanted to use my love for bacon and pralines.

SPIRITS

Agua Bendita
Holy Water

Courtesy of Carolina Hernandez

Ingredients

2 shots of coconut rum

1 shot of vodka

⅓ cup of pineapple juice

⅓ cup of white cranberry juice

⅓ cup of white grapefruit juice

⅓ cup of tonic water

Crushed ice

Preparation

Combine all ingredients in a large cocktail shaker. Add crushed ice. Pour into a glass and garnish with white grapes on a cocktail skewer.

Sangria de los Martin
The Martins' Sangria

Ingredients

1 quart of dry red wine

⅓ cup of brandy

2 large oranges, squeezed

2 lemons, squeezed

4 tablespoons of sugar

6 lemons and oranges, sliced

Preparation

Into a large pitcher pour red wine, brandy, and juice of squeezed oranges and lemons. Add sugar. Adjust sweetness by adding more sugar to preference. Add sliced lemons and oranges to the sangria. Serve.

¡Viva New Orleans!
Daiquiri

Courtesy of Shana Donahue, Rio Mar bartender

Ingredients

3 ripe strawberries

3 peeled cucumber slices

2 large basil leaves

1 tablespoon of superfine sugar

2 ounces of Old New Orleans Crystal Rum

¾ ounce of Luxardo

2 ounces of fresh lime juice

Preparation

Combine strawberries, cucumbers, basil, and sugar in a chilled glass. Muddle ingredients. Into a cocktail shaker put crushed ice, rum, Luxardo, and lime juice. Shake. Strain the drink into the chilled glass.

New Orleans has a long history of mixed cocktail drinks, starting with the Sazerac, the first American cocktail, created by Antoine Amédée Peychaud, who was born in Haiti to French parents who resettled in New Orleans during the Haitian revolution, according to some historians. The import of rum from Cuba during the eighteenth century possibly was the igniting force that developed the drinking culture in New Orleans. New Orleans folklore tells many stories of drunken pirates running amuck in the Vieux Carré (French Quarter). Inside the Southern Food & Beverage Museum in New Orleans, the Museum of the American Cocktail tells the story of how the American cocktail evolved with special attention to New Orleans cocktail history. In Latin America, specifically in Cuba, the daiquiri, a Taíno word, originated reportedly by an American expatriate named Jennings Cox at the turn of the nineteenth century, is a cocktail that both Cuba and New Orleans share to this day. Three people contributed to this section: Carolina Hernandez, New Orleans architect and daughter of Carlos Hernandez, makes agua bendita, or holy water, cocktails often for family functions, the Martins' sangria is a family recipe that was passed down from Mike Martin's father, and Shana Donahue, bartender at Chef Adolfo Garcia's Rio Mar, created a new drink called ¡Viva New Orleans! Daiquiri.

Resources

Creole/Cajun
Cajun Seasoning
Joe's Stuff or K-Paul's
New Orleans School of Cooking
www.neworleansschoolofcooking.com

Crawfish Tails, Live Crawfish, Boudin, and Gulf Shrimp
Cajun Grocer
www.cajungrocer.com

Adobo Seasoning and Beans
Cuban Food Market
www.cubanfoodmarket.com

Spanish Chorizo and Cured Ham
Amigo Foods
www.amigofoods.com

Chiles, Media Crema, Tamale Husks, Tamaleras
Mex Grocer
www.mexgrocer.com

Root vegetables and any other Latin American food products can be found at your local Hispanic grocery store. Do a Google search of Latin grocery stores in your area, come with a prepared written grocery list, and practice your Spanish. ¡Buen Provecho!

Works Cited

Acurio, Gastón. *500 Años De Fusión: La Historia, Los Ingredientes Y Las Nuevas Propuestas De La Cocina Peruana*. Lima: El Comercio, 2008. Print.

Adams, Jeremy duQuesnay. *Multicultural New Orleans: An Historical Sketch*. Lafayette, LA: University of Louisiana at Lafayette, 2001. Print.

Benge, Dorothy L., and Laura M. Sullivan. *Los Isleños Cookbook: Canary Island Recipes: Recipes from Spanish Louisiana*. Gretna, LA: Pelican Pub., 2000. Print.

Berry, Jason, Jonathan Foose, and Tad Jones. *Up from the Cradle of Jazz: New Orleans Music Since World War II*. Athens: University of Georgia Press, 1986. Print.

Chapman, Peter. *Bananas: How the United Fruit Company Shaped the World*. Edinburgh: Canongate, 2007. Print.

Clark, John. *New Orleans, 1718–1812: An Economic History*. New Orleans, LA: Pelican, 1982. Print.

Creen, Linette. *A Taste of Cuba: Recipes From the Cuban-American Community*. New York, NY: Plume, 1994. Print.

The Creole Cookery Book. New Orleans, LA: Christian Woman's Exchange, 1974. Print.

Delgadillo, Rafael. "A 'Spanish' Element in the New South: The Hispanic Press and Community in 19th Century New Orleans." Thesis. New Orleans, LA: University of New Orleans, 2009. Print.

Euraque, Samantha. "Honduran Memories: Identity, Race, Place and Memory in New Orleans, Louisiana." Thesis. Baton Rouge, LA: Louisiana State University, 2004. Web. http://etd.lsu.edu/docs/available/etd-04152004-123822/unrestricted/Euraque_thesis.pdf.

Folse, John D. *The Encyclopedia of Cajun & Creole Cuisine*. Gonzales, LA: Chef John Folse & Pub., 2004. Print.

Garvey, Joan B., and Mary Lou Widmer. *Beautiful Crescent: A History of New Orleans*. New Orleans, LA: Garmer, 1988. Print.

Gehman, Mary. "The Mexico-Louisiana Creole Connection." *Louisiana Cultural Vistas* (2001). *Margaret Media, Inc.* Web. http://margaretmedia.com/index.php?_a=viewDoc&docId=26.

Goodman, Amy. "Honduran Immigrants in New Orleans: Fleeing Hurricanes Mitch, Katrina and Now the U.S. Government." *Democracy Now*. New York, NY, 13 Sept. 2005. Web. http://www.democracynow.org/2005/9/13/honduran_immigrants_in_new_orleans_fleeing.

Gruesz, Kirsten Silva. *Ambassadors of Culture: The Transamerican Origins of Latino Writing*. Princeton, NJ: Princeton University Press, 2002. Print.

Hearn, Lafcadio, and William Head Coleman. *La Cuisine Creole. A Collection of Culinary Recipes From Leading Chefs and Noted Creole Housewives, Who Have Made New Orleans Famous for Its Cuisine*. New York, NY: W. H. Coleman, 1885. Print.

Hearn, Lafcadio. *Lafcadio Hearn's Creole Cook Book*. Gretna, LA: Pelican Pub., 1990. Print.

Hernandez, Mayra. "Best Jibarito Sandwiches In Chicago." *Huffington Post*. 15 Dec. 2010. Web. http://www.huffingtonpost.com/2010/12/14/best-jibarito-sandwiches-_n_796787.html#s206305&title=Borinquen_Lounge_1720.

Huse, Andrew. "Welcome to Cuban Sandwich City." *Tampa Bay's Cigar City Magazine*. 14 Jan. 2011. Web. http://www.cigarcitymagazine.com/food/item/welcome-to-cuban-sandwich-city.

"Immigration Matters: Mexican Strawberry Pickers Seek African American Help—NAM." *New America Media*. Web. 07 Feb. 2012. http://news.newamericamedia.org/news/view_article.html?article_id=5149558d7e6e6f80a15cafd1586bd8c5.

Janer, Zilkia. *Latino Food Culture.* Westport, CT: Greenwood, 2008. Print.

Kelman, Ari. *A River and Its City: The Nature of Landscape in New Orleans.* Berkeley: University of California Press, 2003. Print.

Kiple, Kenneth F. *A Movable Feast: Ten Millennia of Food Globalization.* Cambridge: Cambridge University Press, 2007. Print.

Laborde, Peggy Scott, and Tom Fitzmorris. *Lost Restaurants of New Orleans.* Gretna: Pelican Pub., 2011. Print.

Leslie, Austin, and Marie Rudd Posey. *Austin Leslie's Creole-Soul: New Orleans Cooking with a Soulful Twist.* Neuchatel: Simonin Pub., 2000. Print.

McDonald, Michael R. *Food Culture in Central America.* Santa Barbara, CA: Greenwood, 2009. Print.

Montero De Pedro, José. *The Spanish in New Orleans and Louisiana.* Gretna, LA: Pelican Pub., 2000. Print.

Moss, Robert F. *Barbecue: The History of an American Institution.* Tuscaloosa: University of Alabama Press, 2010. Print.

Nazario, Luis Adam. *Mi Vida Estudiantil En Nueva Orleans.* Rio Piedras, P.R.: Editorial Edil, 1971. Print.

Nott, William. "Impresiones De Nueva Orleans: Una Ciudad Latina Dentro De Los Estados Unidos." *Lucero Latino: Revista Mensual* 23.

Ochoa Gautier, Ana Maria. "Nueva Orleans, La Permeable Margen Norte Del Caribe." *Nueva Sociedad 201* Feb. 2006: 61–72. Print.

O'Toole, G. J. A. *The Spanish War, An American Epic—1898.* New York, NY: Norton, 1984. Print.

Painter, Norman Wellington. "The Assimilation of Latin Americans in New Orleans, Louisiana." Thesis. New Orleans, LA: Tulane University, 1949. Print.

Perez, Samantha. *The Isleños of Louisiana: On the Water's Edge.* Charleston, SC: History, 2011. Print.

The Picayune's Creole Cook Book. New York: Weathervane, 1989. Print.

Rose, Al. *Storyville, New Orleans, Being an Authentic, Illustrated Account of the Notorious Red-Light District.* University: University of Alabama Press, 1974. Print.

Scott, Rebecca J. *Degrees of Freedom: Louisiana and Cuba after Slavery.* Cambridge, MA: Belknap Press of Harvard University Press, 2008. Print.

Southern Food & Beverage Museum. *New Orleans con Sabor Latino Exhibit.* Tulane University. Aug. 2010. Web. http://stonecenter.tulane.edu/articles/detail/586/New-Orleans-con-Sabor-Latino.

Starr, S. Frederick, ed. *Inventing New Orleans: Writings of Lafcadio Hearn.* Jackson: University Press of Mississippi, 2001. Print.

Tucker, Susan. *New Orleans Cuisine: Fourteen Signature Dishes and Their Histories.* Jackson: University Press of Mississippi, 2009. Print.

Walker, Judy. "Manuel Hernandez and Family Made Local Culinary History." *Times-Picayune* [New Orleans, LA], 28 Aug. 2008. Print.

Index